AMAZON FIRE HD 10 TABLET USER MANUAL 2022

Complete Step by Step Guide On How to Use and Mastering My All-New Kindle Fire HD 10 11th Generation Tablet.

Will Dwight

Copyright@2022 All Right Reserved: The content in this book may not be reproduced, transcribe, photocopy, or transmitted without due permission from the publisher or the author.

With no account will any blame or liability be held against the author for any slow learning, lack of performance, or loss in monetary terms due to information contained in this book.

Legal Notice:

This publication is copyright protected and intended for personal use only with no means of plagiarizing, lifting, or reproduce to be resold as a different book.

Disclaimer Notice:

Please the information in this book is for educational and entertainment use only. All sincere practice has been put in place to produce correct, relevant, updated, and reliable information. The content contained in this book has been gotten from various sources of knowledge and all techniques highlighted have been put to practice. Using this document adheres readers to comply that no liability is held against the author for any direct or indirect incurred as a result of the informational content. But no limitation to possible errors, inaccuracies, and mistakes.

Table of Contents

Introduction 8

Chapter 1: Overview of The All-New Amazon HD 10 Tablet Features 10

    The Alternatives Within the Fire HD 10 Range Are Wider Than Expected..11

    AMAZON FIRE HD 10 13

        Top Notch Features of Fire HD 10 14

        Draw Backs of Fire HD 10 14

    AMAZON FIRE HD 10 PLUS PRODUCTIVITY BUNDLE............19

    AMAZON FIRE HD 10 KIDS AND HD 10 KIDS PRO................22

        Advantage..23

    Disadvantage 23

    AGREEMENT: AMAZON FIRE HD 10 (2021) 26

Chapter 2: Get Started (Examine the Tablet, Prepare your device)..27

    Storage 27

    Sound 27

    Bezel 27

    Internal Specification 27

    Hardware 28

    Battery 28

    The screen..28

Chapter 3: Internal Features and Operational Guide 30

    The unique features of All-New Fire HD 10................30

Chapter 4: Operational Guide 32

Lock or Unlock Your Device.. 32
    How to Lock Your Device?.. 32
    How to Unlock Your Device?... 32
How to fix likely startup issues 32
Charge Using AC Adapter 33
How to Restore Latest Software? 33
How to Restart Your Tablet?... 33
    How to Restart a Fire Tablet with the Power Button?..... 33
How to Force a Reboot on a Fire Tablet? 34
How to Set Up Your Device? 34
How to Set an Email Address? 44
Advanced Email Security Port Settings................................ 45
How to Transfer Content from Your Computer?................ 46
How to find the User Guide? 49
How to Change the Screen Brightness?............................... 50
How to Change the Screen Timeout? 50
How to Increase And Decrease the Volume? 51
How to Take Screenshots?... 52
How to use the Camera?.. 52
How to Clear Browser History?.. 53
How to Enable Split-Screen?.. 56
How to Install Software Updates? 58
How to Disable Safe Mode?... 63
Chapter 5: HD 10 Tablet Connectivity 64
    How to Connect to The Internet (Wifi On Your Tablet) 64
    Manual Wifi Setup... 65

How to Fix the Authentication Problem?.............................. 66

How to Set Time/Date?... 67

How to Reset the Router?... 67

How to Browse with Your HD 10? 68

How to Use the Amazon AppStore? 68

How to Customize Bluetooth Keyboard Shortcuts?................ 70

Chapter 6: Registration Of Your New Device 71

How to Register the Widget on Your Amazon Account? 71

How to Pass a Two-step Verification? 72

How to Change Your Device Name? 73

Chapter 7: Charging... 75

How to Wirelessly Charge Your Device?................................. 75

How to Fix Possible Wireless Charging Issues? 75

How to Solve a Liquid Detection Alert?.................................. 76

Chapter 8: Applications... 78

How to Fix Possible App Errors 78

How to Force Close An App?... 78

How to Clean An App's Data And Cache................................ 78

How to Move an App On the Screen? 79

How to Download the Hoopla App?....................................... 79

How to Install Tiktok App?.. 79

How to Download an App on Google Playstore? 83

Chapter 9: Game Mode.. 84

How to Enable Game Mode?.. 84

How to Disable Game Mode ? 84

Chapter 10: Print 85

How to Print From Your Device? 85
How to Add a Printer Manually? 85
Chapter 11: Amazon Kindle Guide 87
How to Download Books from the Amazon Library? 87
Chapter 12: Battery 88
How Tt Conserve Battery Power? 88
What is Smart Suspend? 88
Chapter 13: Household Profiles 90
How to Create a Child Profile? 90
Chapter 14: Parental Control 97
How to Enable Parental Control? 98
How to Adjust Communication Features? 98
How to Approve Contact for Your Child? 99
Chapter 15: Data Storage 100
How to run microSD on your Tablet? 100
How to Delete all Data from Your SD Card? 101
Chapter 16: Alexa 102
How to use Device Dashboard? 102
How to Connect Smart Home Devices to Alexa? 102
How to use Alexa on Your Tablet? 103
How to Enable Alexa Hands-free? 103
How to Permanently Disable Alexa? 104
How to Switch to Show Mode? 104
Chapter 17: Data Reset 106
How to Reset Your Tablet to Factory Setting? 106
How to Soft Reset Your Tablet? 108

6 | P a g e

How to Reset Lock Screen Password or Parental Controls PIN? 108

Chapter 18: ADS 113

How to Remove Ads from Your Tablet? 113

Chapter 19: Troubleshooting Tips & Tips 117

Conclusion 121

Introduction

The Fire HD 10 (2021) is the 11th gen update to Amazon's Fire HD 10 line and the fourth 10.1-inch Tablet launched by the company.

PORTS, BUTTONS & COLORS

- 5 MP rear-facing HD camera
- Volume buttons
- Power button
- 2 built-in Microphones
- Color
- 2 MP front-facing camera
- 3.5mm stereo jack
- 2 built-in microphones
- volume buttons
- USB-C (2.0) port
- Power button

The device successes the 2019's 9th gen Amazon Fire HD 10 and is the most rated amazon tablet after the Fire HD 10 Plus, which is also 10.1-inches in size.

The Plus has an extra 1GB RAM compared with the Fire HD 10, supporting Qi wireless charging. Some functions are the same in both tablets, such as the processor, battery life, storage options, cameras, and size are consistent across the HD 10 line.

- The back of the Tablet is matte plastic which appears cheap but is quite durable. Fire HD 10 are Black, Denim, Olive, and Lavender.
- The display is okay; the Images are sharp with vibrant colors. HD videos also come out nice, and you can use them to stream films like TV and make video calls.
- The Fire HD 10 is based on Amazon's Fire OS. It comes with a high number of Amazon apps.
- The Fire HD 10 is powered by an octa-core processor and has a RAM of 3GB and a storage of 32GB or 64GB, which can be expanded up to 1TB with micro SD.
- The Battery can stream video for more than 7 hours and charges to 100% in about 4hours.
- The Fire HD 10 is the default model, and the one most people should choose.

Chapter 1: Overview of The All-New Amazon HD 10 Tablet Features

Amazon's lineup of Fire tablets is available in small, medium, and large; they are priced far lower than comparable iPads. They are great for reading and watching movies or TV; Amazon supplies the contents. The company does not update them regularly; sometimes, it takes years before upgrading. Usually, the update remains the same. The Fire HD 10 tablet is nice and cheap; it is a good source of content from Amazon and is used for studying Kindle books, Prime Video movies and TV shows, and Audible audiobooks. It also has access to other streaming services, like Netflix, Disney Plus, Hulu, and HBO Max. There are also Kids' editions by which parents can limit what content their children have access to or how long they can use a screen each day. Fire HD 10 cannot be used as a replacement for your laptop or when performing severe work.

The Alternatives Within the Fire HD 10 Range Are Wider Than Expected

The Fire HD 10 family has a lot of alternatives, including the $150 standard model, the $180 Fire HD 10 Plus, a $200 HD 10 Kids model, and a $200 HD 10 Kids Pro option. The hardware of the Fire HD 10, the Fire HD 10 Kids, and the Fire HD 10 Kids Pro are alike; the Fire HD 10 Plus has more RAM gigabyte, a soft-touch finish, and wireless charging.

The Fire HD 10 and 10 Plus storages are 32GB or 64GB; the Kids models are 32GB. They all support the use of Micro SD card storage expansion up to 1TB. Four muted color options are available in the Fire HD 10, while the 10 Plus only comes in black, and the Kids versions come with different colorful cases. By default, Amazon's lock screen ads are included in the HD 10 and 10 Plus.

More configuration options were added by Amazon for the Fire HD 10 and also increased the number of accessories you can select from. A $50 detachable keyboard case can be used with the Fire HD 10 or 10 Plus. It is available in a "Productivity Bundle" this includes the Tablet, the keyboard case, and a year of Microsoft 365 for $220 or $250, according to the Fire HD 10 you select. A $40 wireless charging dock is also available; Anker produces specially designed for the Fire HD 10 Plus and changes it into an Alexa bright display. A standard suite of $40 is also available; it has color-matched snap-on cases that function with either model and provide protection and a vertical or horizontal kickstand.

AMAZON FIRE HD 10

The Fire HD 10 is the default model, and the one most people should choose.

The latest Fire HD 10 lineup is more improved than 2019: the faceplate around the screen is now uniform; this makes it easy to hold and gives it a more modern look than before. The faceplates on the long side are slightly more prominent, but those on the short sides are smaller than before, with the net effect being a noticeably smaller overall footprint. The edges are now more rounded, giving it a more iPad-like silhouette, and it's about eight percent lighter, tipping the scales at just over a pound. It has a rugged plastic chassis that looks cheap, but the finish masks any fingerprints.

According to the company, inside the smaller faceplates is a 10.1-inch 1080p display that is 10 percent brighter than the previous model. The screen is sharp, has good color and saturation, and works well indoors. It's not nice in direct sunlight — a 10 percent brightness bump or not — and it cannot compare to the best displays from Samsung or Apple, but it is okay considering the price.

Top Notch Features of Fire HD 10

- It is cheap
- The screen is sharp and colorful
- Increased Performance
- Better battery life

Draw Backs of Fire HD 10
- The software feels old.
- The stylus support on the Fire HD 10 models is inactive. So you cannot take notes on the screen or create artwork. If that's a feature you desire, this isn't the best deal for you.

- A USB-C port is used for charging, while a 3.5mm headphone jack is used for audio.

- Behind the Fire HD 10, a hard plastic does not show fingerprints and is high quality.

- Amazon adjusted the front-facing camera from the short edge, similar to iPads, to the long edge, so video calls in landscape orientation are more elegant. The 2-megapixel camera is not the best. It has lots of image noise, smeared details, and low color saturation, same with the upgraded 5-megapixel camera on the back. It works well for scanning the occasional document, but other phones might work better.

- Within the latest Fire HD 10, a similar 2GHz octa-core MediaTek MT8183 processor is within the previous model. But presently, it is combined with 3GB of RAM (an increase of 50 percent), which provides a clear improvement in the performance of the Tablet. Apps open fast, and the navigation between home screens and menus is faster and easier to operate.

- Amazon says the Battery lasts up to 12 hours, and it takes 4 hours to completely recharge the Tablet with the 9W charging brick, which is included. This time can be shortened by using a faster charger; a 30W USB-C charger will take 2 hours to charge the Tablet.

- Amazon did not alter the speaker with two speakers on the top edge (when handling the Tablet in landscape orientation). A 3.5mm jack and Bluetooth support to use any headphones you desire.
- The best feature of the Fire HD 10 is its display, which is excellent for a $150 tablet.
- One other thing Amazon has not changed in a long time is the software. The Fire HD 10 controls the company's Fire OS fork of Android, the most recent version based on the years-old Android 9 platform. It makes it appear old when compared to a more recent Android phone. Gesture-based interfaces are not present, a light mode and dark mode to automatically switch in the software or some other functions we are used to in the latest Android versions are absent.
- Amazon utilizes the home screen to promote content, apps, videos, and many others more in a spam way when you are in an actual app; this spam fade away.
- Amazon does not have access to the Google Play Store and therefore lacks many of the apps you are used to on the phone, such as Gmail, YouTube, Google Maps, Google Docs, etc. Amazon's Appstore is not well-stocked and lacks the latest, most popular apps and games. This won't be a problem if all you

want to do on the Tablet is watch movies or TV shows. But you can find a way out in this guide on how to install your preferred app.

AMAZON FIRE HD 10 PLUS PRODUCTIVITY BUNDLE

The Productivity Bundle consists of a detachable keyboard and a year of Microsoft 365 so that apps like Word can be used in split-screen on the Fire HD 10.

The Fire HD 10 Plus is similar to the standard model but with 4GB of RAM instead of 3GB, a soft-touch finish, and wireless charging.

Fintie forms the keyboard case, but it is designed like the Fire HD 10. A detachable Bluetooth keyboard pairs wirelessly with the Tablet in one half of it and a snap-on case on the other half. It connects to the keyboard through magnets to form a familiar clamshell look. The keyboard can easily be detached when not in use.

The keyboard is small and made of plastic.

The Fire HD 10 Plus has a soft-touch finish at the back.

The keyboard is small, has no backlight, and the keys are plastic. There is no function row for media controls, brightness, and volume, and it has a shortcut for opening the

Fire HD 10's split-screen mode so that two apps can function at once. It lacks a trackpad or pointing device.

This problem can be combated by sideloading the Google Play Store and its services to the Fire HD. Still, you need to disable security features, download software from sites not authorized to distribute it, and install it in a specific order.

When you get all the apps, you desire in the Appstore, you might have issues using them in split-screen mode. When this arises, you have to exit the split-screen mode. The Tablet has a small screen and a widescreen aspect ratio, making things relatively small to work with when you have two apps open.

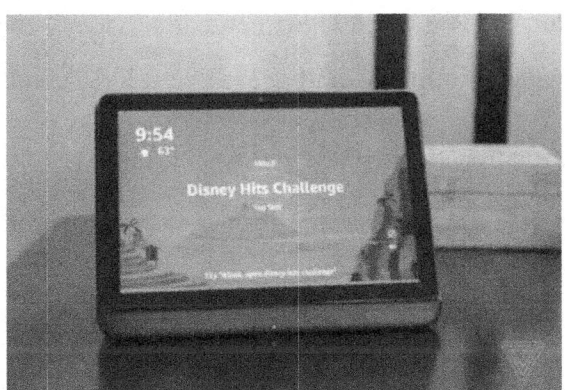

AMAZON FIRE HD 10 KIDS AND HD 10 KIDS PRO

The Kids version of the Fire HD 10 has two different models for various age groups.

Like older Kids' versions, the new models come with a year's subscription to Amazon's Kids Plus content service, a two-year warranty against damage, and a case that is kid-friendly.

Regardless of the names, the Kids and Kids Pro have similar hardware but different cases.

The Kids model is designed by amazon for ages 3 to 7 and comes with a chunky, spongy rubber case that little hands can hold on to and protects the Tablet from tumbles and drops. The Kids Pro version is designed for children ages 6 to 12 and comes with a slimmer plastic case that's more akin to a standard tablet case. Both cases come in different colors and designs and built-in kickstands that carry handles.

Advantage
- Good parental controls / content library
- It comes with a damage protection plan
- Easy software for kids to use

Disadvantage
- Not the best for schoolwork
- Lacks active stylus support
- Limited Internal Storage

One thing that did not change is the home screen and app grid on the HD 10 Kids, but the HD 10 Kids Pro has a cleaner interface like that of a phone, with a search bar at the top and more mature app icons. This new interface is determined by the age range you pick for your child's profile, not the hardware; you could put the new interface on the standard Kids tablet if you want to.

The Kids model cases have a built-in kickstand that can also handle.

USB-C port is used for charging, which is much easier to handle than the Micro USB port on prior tablets.

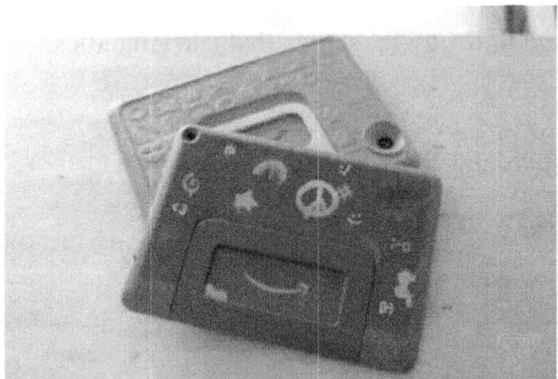

The Kids version for younger children has a chunky, spongy case; the model for older kids has a slimmer plastic one.

The Tablet for younger kids does not have a web browser, and parents can regulate camera use. For older kids, a web browser with built-in content filters is available. Parents can also turn this off. Apps not present in Amazon's Kids Plus library can be requested and enabled for the kids' profiles.

All of this can be regulated by parents, plus the screen time limits, from a web dashboard on any device, making it easier to manage. You can set it up and then hand it over to your kid without worrying about what they are accessing or who they might be communicating with. Personalized profiles accessible right from the lock screen can also be created if more than one kid uses a single tablet.

AGREEMENT: AMAZON FIRE HD 10 (2021)

All smart devices require you to agree to a set of terms and conditions before you can utilize it

To use the Fire HD 10, you have to log in with an Amazon account. You also have to agree to Amazon's mandatory "Conditions of Use" agreement, including eight different compulsory terms of use. The agreement is carried out at once.

Chapter 2: Get Started (Examine the Tablet, Prepare your device)

Storage
Amazon Fire HD 10 tablet is available in 32 and 64 GB models. This can be expanded by adding a microSD card, up to 256 GB, to add high-quality movies and TV shows.

Sound
The Fire HD 10 has dual speakers with the branding of Dolby Atmos. It has a peak volume of 84dB, and it comes with Bluetooth 4.2 and a headphone jack for different listening options.

Bezel
The Fire HD 10 now looks much more like a modern tablet, with a simple design and slimmed-down bezels 15mm thick on all four sides of the screen.

Internal Specification
- Brand - Amazon
- Model - Fire HD 10
- Dimensions (mm)   262.00 x 159.00 x 7.70
- Weight (g) - 432.00
    - Removable battery - No

- Display
- Screen size (inches) - 10.10
- Touchscreen - No
- Resolution - 1280x800

Hardware
Processor - 1.2GHz quad-core
Processor make   MediaTek
RAM - 1GB

Battery
The Fire HD 10 has a 6,300mAh battery. It would last more than 8 hours to stream high-definition video over Wi-Fi at full brightness.

The screen
Fire HD 10 has a widescreen 1280 x 800 high definition display with more than a million pixels (149 PPI) for a bright, vivid picture. You would enjoy a pleasant viewing experience with large angles, reduced glare, blacker blacks, and more brightness due to the highly laminated IPS (in-plane switching) LCD.

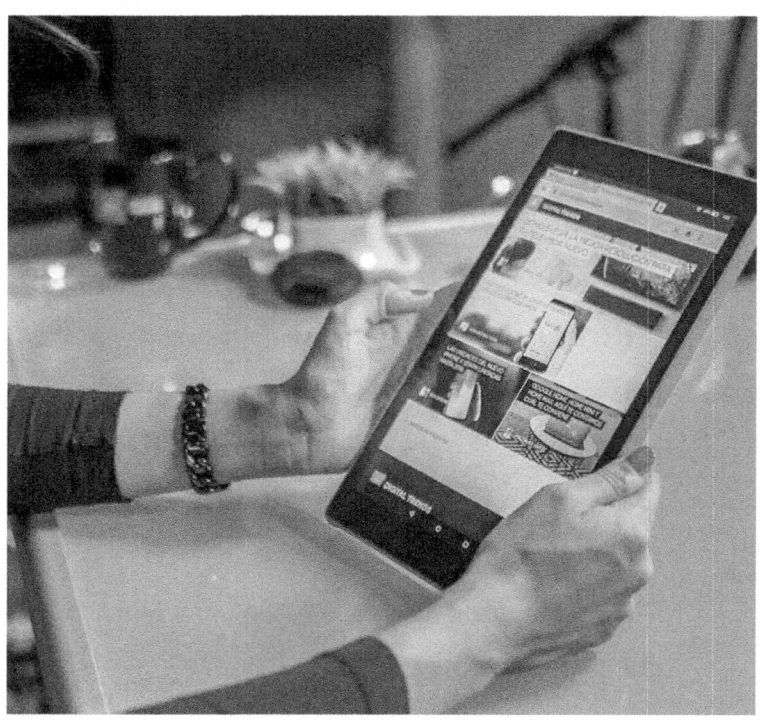

Chapter 3: Internal Features and Operational Guide

The unique features of All-New Fire HD 10

1. It has a beautiful display giving a bright and clear image quality.
2. A faster processor—With an octa-core 2.0 GHz processor and 2 GB RAM, easily switch between apps, stream movies, and browse the web.
3. The Battery lasts for a long —Up to 12 hours before going off.
4. High storage capacity of 32 or 64 GB, and up to 512 GB of expandable Storage through microSD.
5. Charges faster and Easier.
6. It has Dual-band Wi-Fi with a higher capacity to stream your favorite videos with more 802.11ac Wi-Fi support.
7. Highly reliable with a durability of 4x that of the latest iPad Pro and is much cheaper.
8. It has a picture-in-picture feature.
9. The Alexa hands-free feature lets you control video and music playback, get news and sports scores, and others.

10. Amazon Free Time by which parents can control their children's activities.

Chapter 4: Operational Guide

Lock or Unlock Your Device
How to Lock Your Device?

1. On your home screen, scroll down to settings out of view.

2. In settings, go to Security & Privacy.

3. Turn on the toggle for Lock Screen Passcode.

4. Select between a PIN or Password at the top, type in the Password/Pin, and then confirm by typing again.

5. Click Finish when completed.

How to Unlock Your Device?

When you wake your device with the power button, it will request the Password or PIN. When you provide it, your phone will automatically unlock

How to fix likely startup issues

1. Hold Power Button: Hold down the "Power" button for 5 seconds to power it on normally. Don't just tap it as this will not turn it on.

Charge Using AC Adapter

Make sure the Battery of your Amazon Fire is charged. Plug the Fire into a wall outlet as power supplied from another device like a computer may not be good enough. Leave the Fire to charge from the wall for at least 20 minutes before you turn it on.

Hold "Volume Down" While Powering On

Holding the "Volume Down" button together with the "Power" for about 5 seconds also works if your Fire doesn't turn on.

How to Restore Latest Software?

Touch and hold the "Volume Up" button with your Fire off, then press "Power" for 45 seconds to turn the Fire on.

Hold the "Volume Up" for some time until you see a message that says, "Installing the latest software. " When you complete the installation, you can enjoy using the device again.

How to Restart Your Tablet?

How to Restart a Fire Tablet with the Power Button?

Locate and hold down the device's physical power button till a menu appears on the screen.

Touch and hold the power button for at least 20 seconds.

Options for "Power Off" and "Restart." will appear.

Tap "Restart."

If the touchscreen is not working, you have to force a reboot.

How to Force a Reboot on a Fire Tablet?

Locate and hold down the power button for 20 seconds and let go of it when the screen goes black. Wait for a little and then press and hold the power button to turn on the Tablet again.

How to Set Up Your Device?

To turn on your Tablet, Press and hold the power button on the top edge of the Tablet.

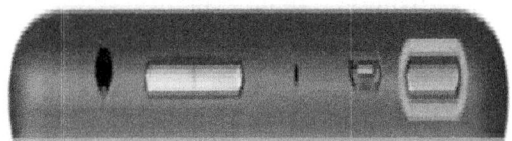

Select the language and location, font size you want, and tap Continue.

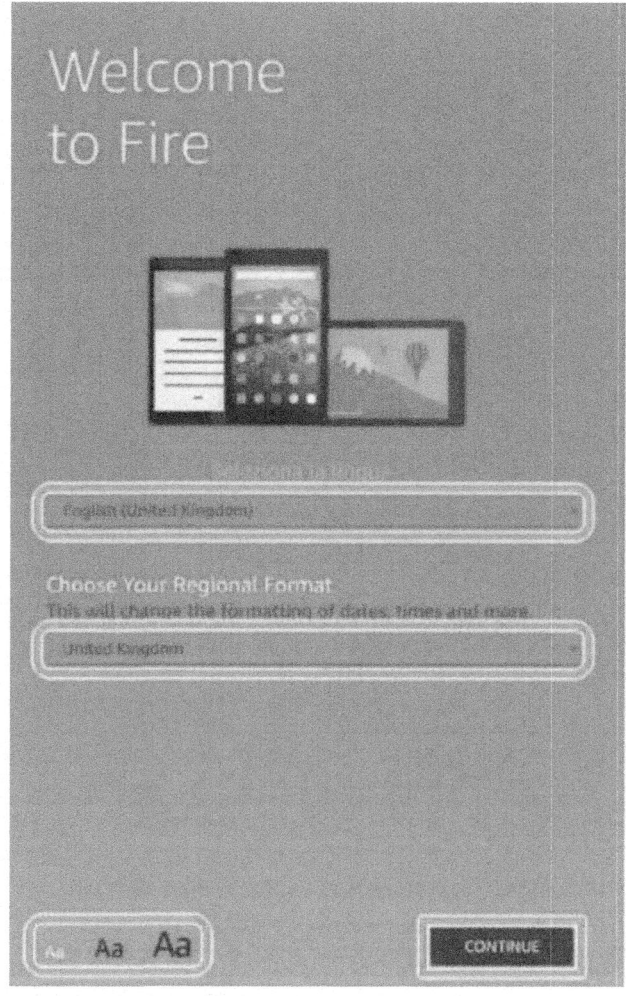

Choose your Wi-Fi network and type in the Wi-Fi password is required to connect your Tablet to the internet.

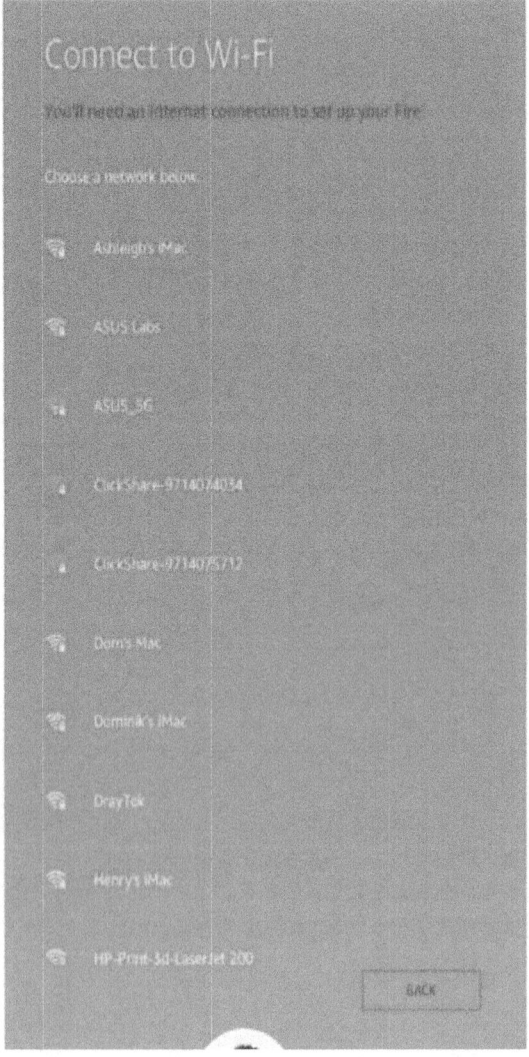

The tablet downloads and installs any updates available.

Register your Tablet in one of these two ways:

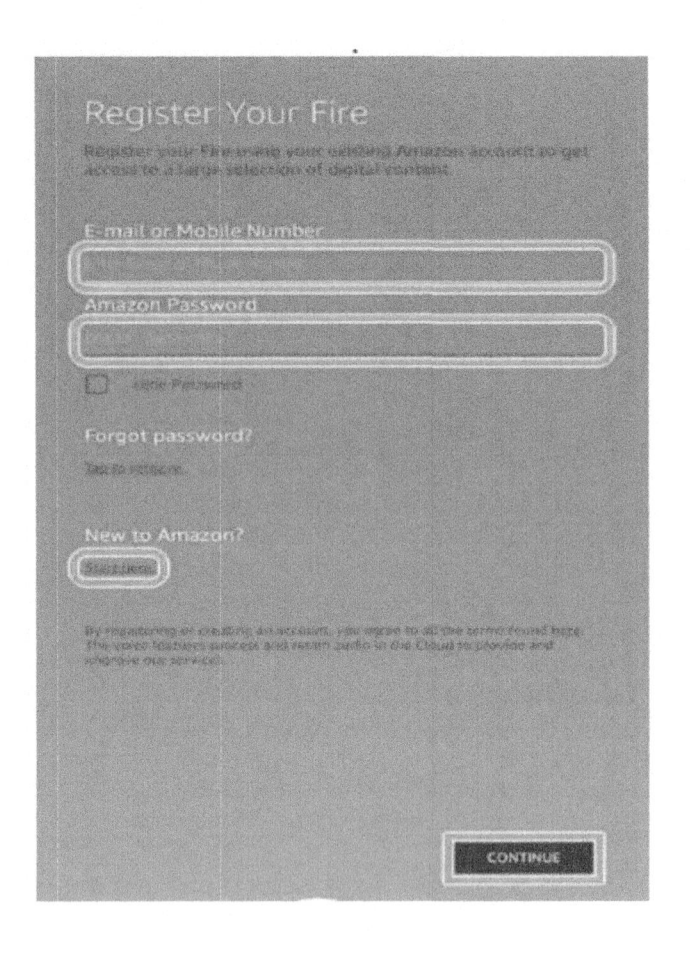

Log in with an existing Amazon account – write your email or mobile number and your account password, then touch Continue,

Create a new Amazon account – touch Start here below the "New to Amazon?" heading, fill out the needed information, and tap Continue.

If you logged in with an existing Amazon account which you have the data backed up, then you can: Touch Restore to load all your apps and settings from your backup,

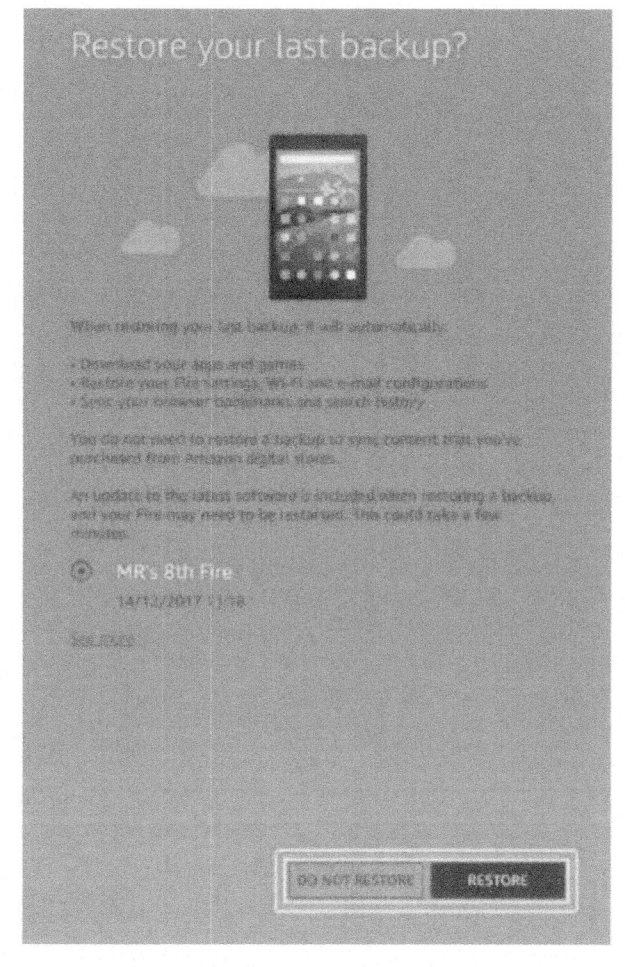

Touch Do Not Restore if you do not want your old information.

Review the options you want to turn on or off, check the ones you want to use, uncheck the ones you don't want to use, and then touch Continue.

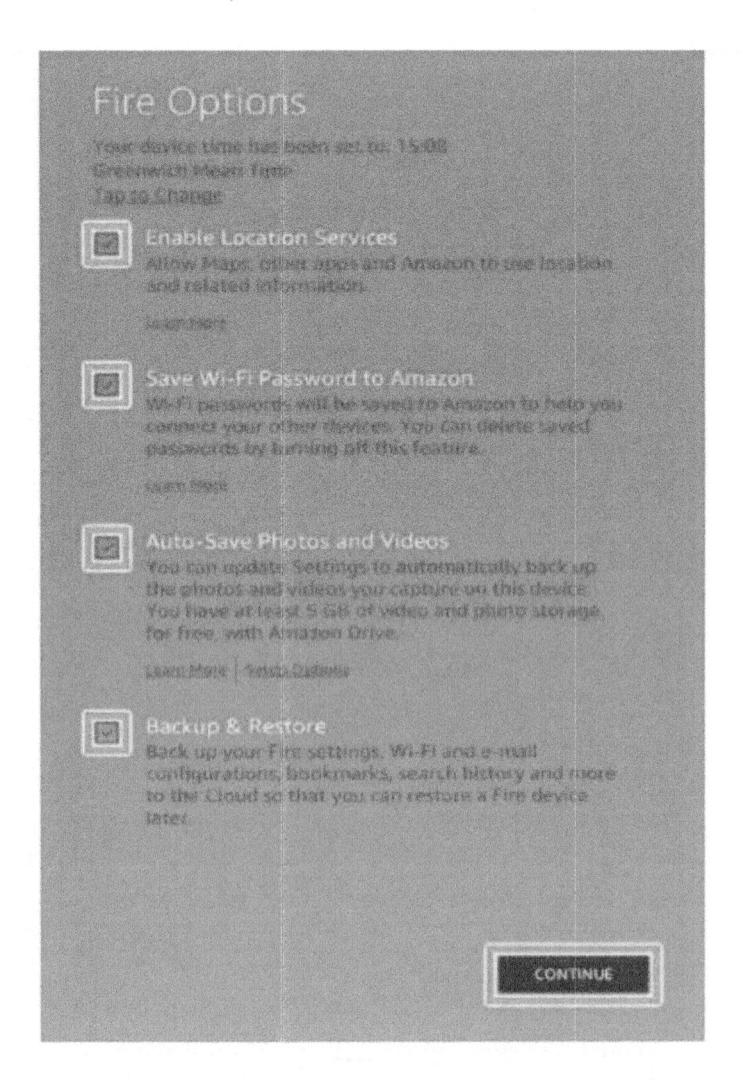

Select the people who will use this Tablet. A child account can also be set up with customized settings for a safer experience. Touch Continue completed.

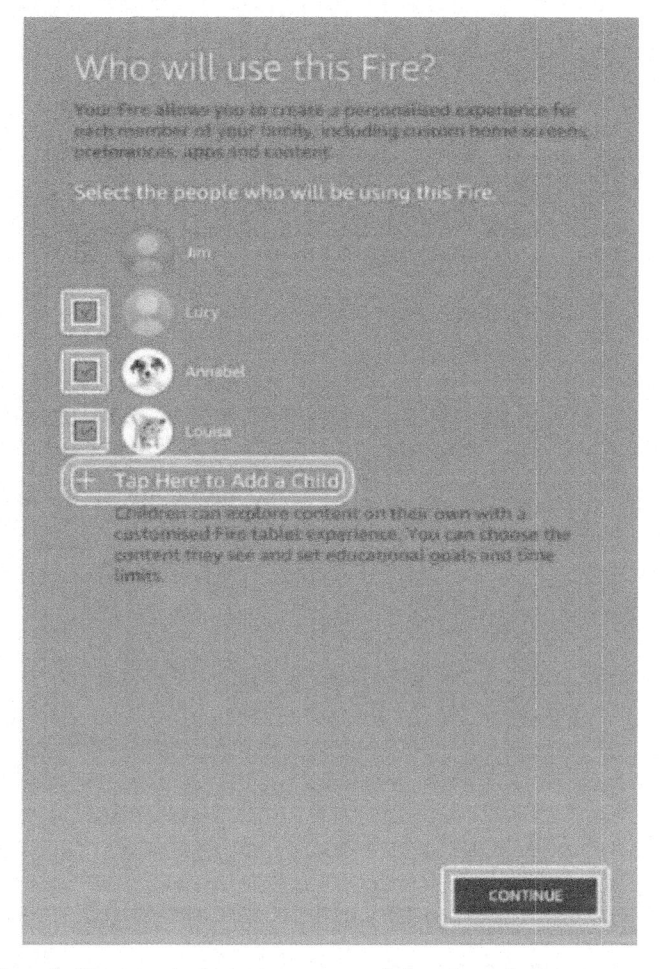

Touch Connect close to any social network you want to utilize on the Tablet, log in with the respective account, and tap Continue.

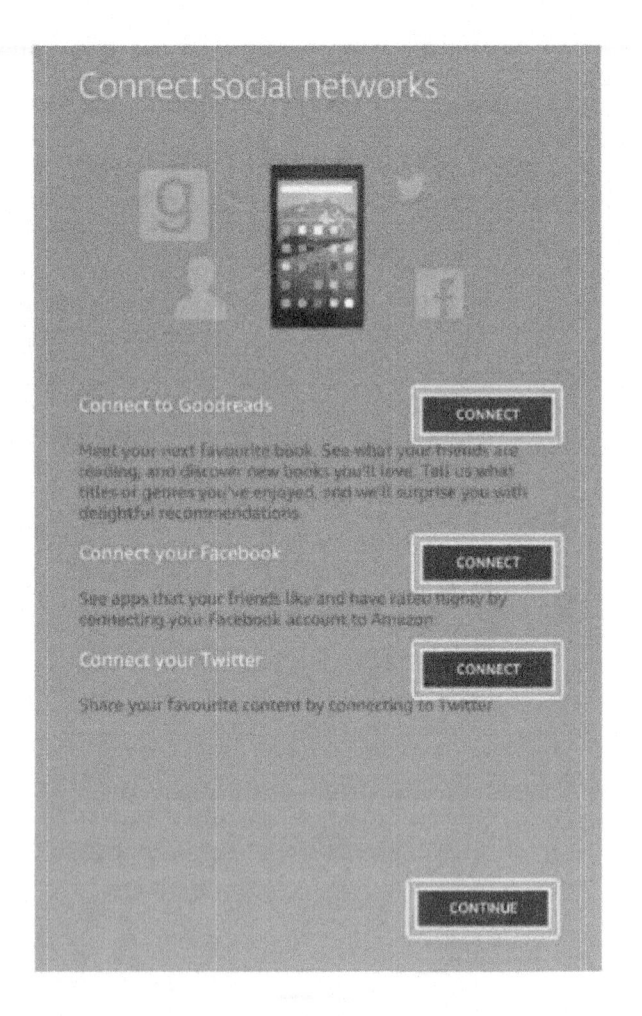

According to services you are subscribed to within your Amazon account, you might receive offers that you can sign up for at this time. You can also decide to proceed without signing up for them.

A list of apps that you can select from to download and Install might also be sent to you.

At this point, the setup will be complete, and you will be welcomed to the tutorial from which you will learn how to use your Tablet.

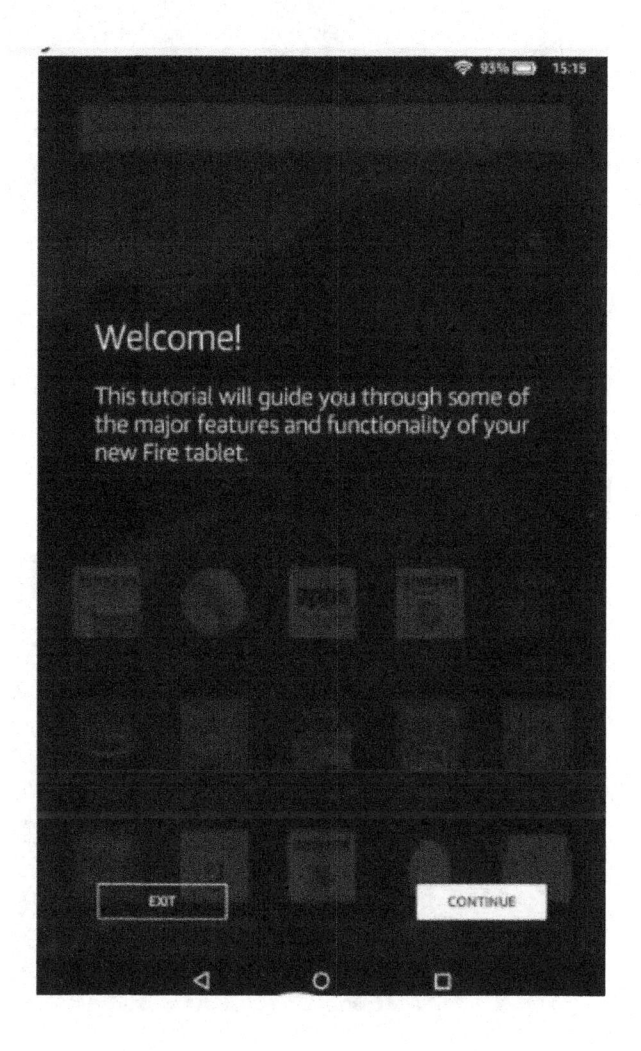

How to Set an Email Address?

Click on the Email app icon to launch it on the home screen.

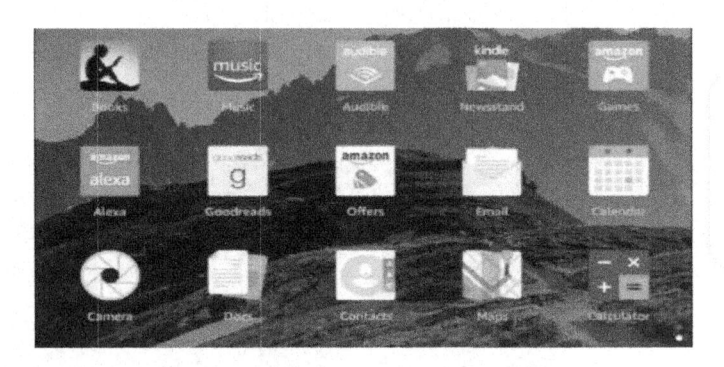

Fire HD Email Icon

If you want to set up a typical web-based email account like Gmail or Microsoft, type in your email address, Password, and click Next.

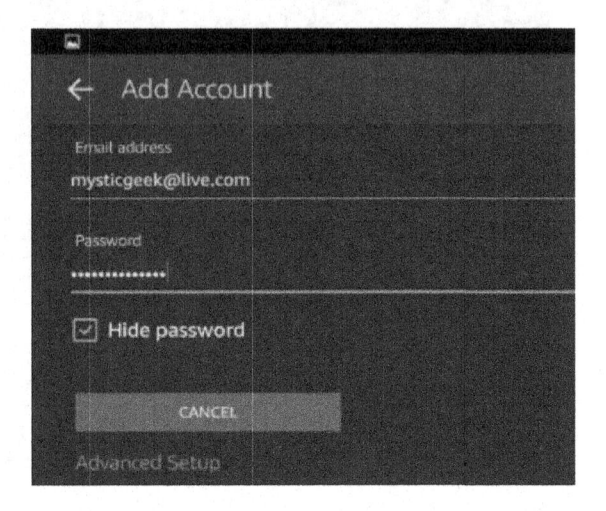

Email and Password

The email app makes advanced setup options available. Which you will use to connect to an Exchange server or if you need to change security and port settings. But if 2FV or 2FA is activated on your email account, you have to use the second verification method the provider uses, like a text to your phone. You might also need to form an app password, like when setting up your Microsoft Emil accounts.

Advanced Email Security Port Settings

The app works exactly like a mobile email when successfully setting up everything. First of all, swipe through a few instructions on using the app.

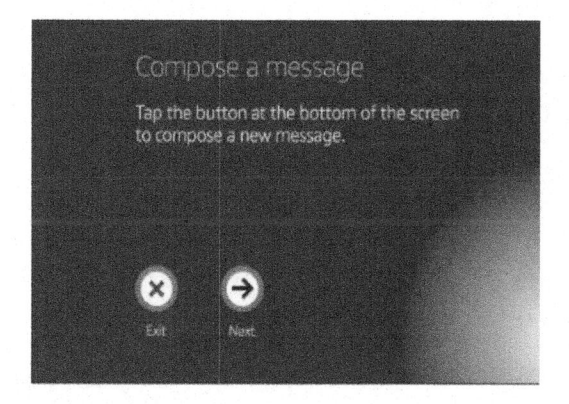

How to Transfer Content from Your Computer?

Connect the device to a computer using a USB cable.

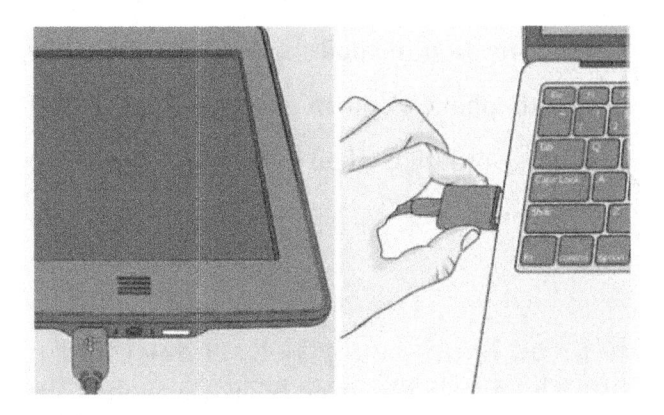

The Fire tablet connects to your computer immediately, and you will notice a popup display showing options to manage the Kindle device.

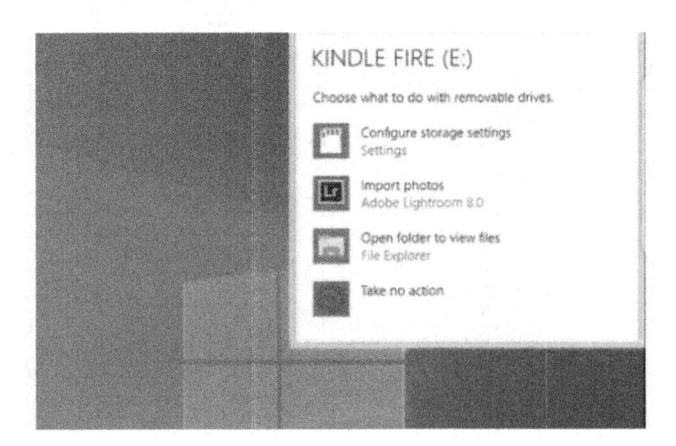

Tap "Open folder to view files.".

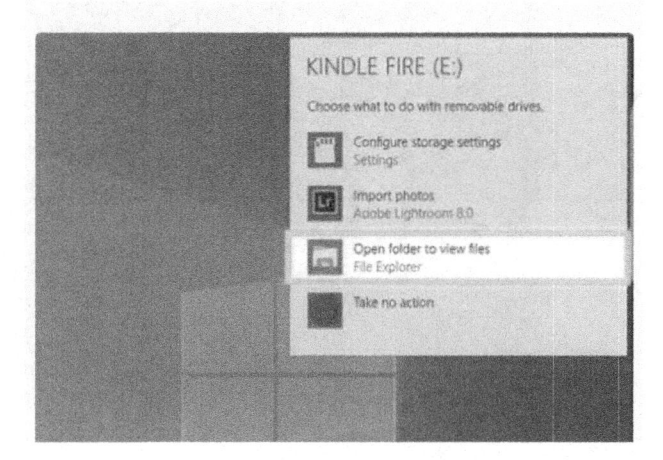

If you do not see this popup, click the icon like a folder in the Task Bar to open Windows Explorer. Then tap Kindle or Fire below "My Computer" or "Computer" in the sidebar towards the left.

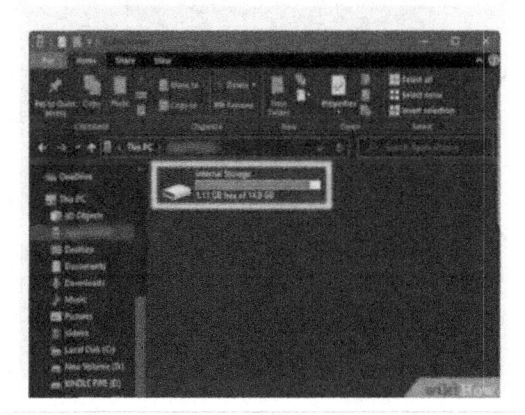

Tap the "Internal Storage" folder.

Click on Disconnect at the base of your Fire screen.

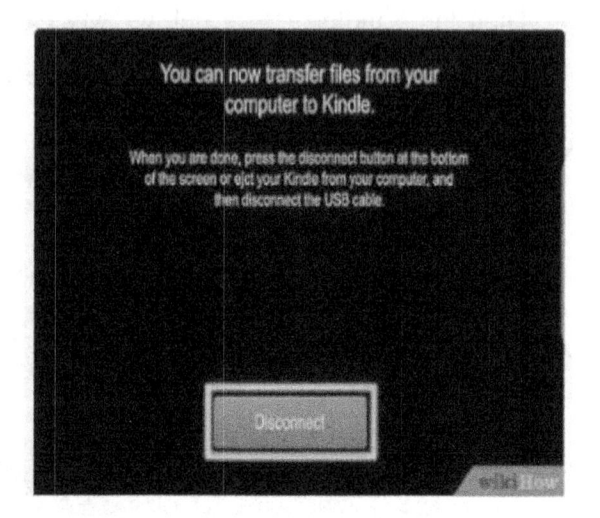

Uninsert the micro-USB cable from your Fire.

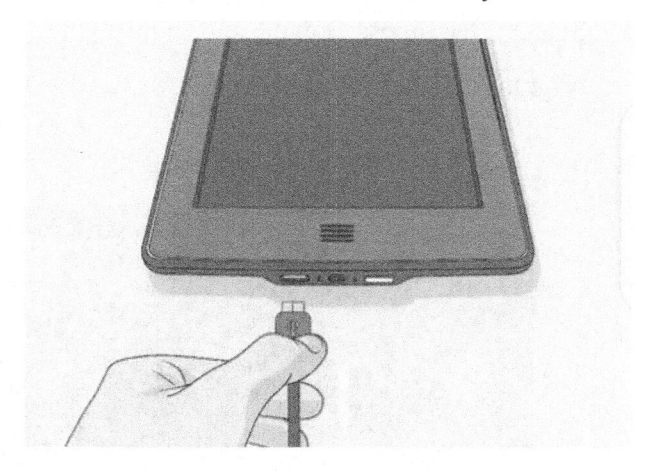

The Fire tablet will show up as a removable disc drive. Windows users can look under "Computer "/" My Computer." At the same time, Mac users can look on the desktop. Open the "KINDLE" drive. You will see a folder named "Pictures. " Try to drag and drop any of your pictures to this folder. An entire folder can also be dragged to the "Pictures" folder, and they will stay organized on the device as well.

How to find the User Guide?
Click on the Settings menu.

Click on Help and then on User Guide.

How to Change the Screen Brightness?

Open the settings menu and select display.

Select Brightness Level and adjust the screen's brightness using the slider.

How to Change the Screen Timeout?

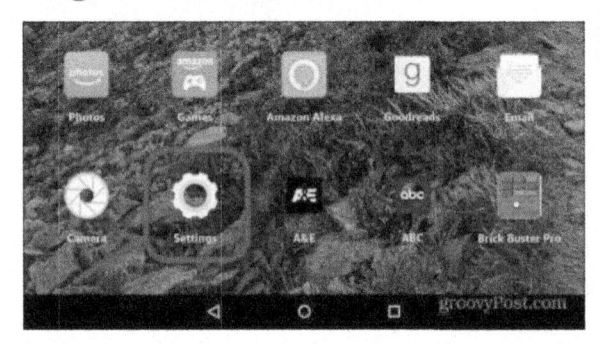

On the settings menu, click on Display or Display & Sounds.

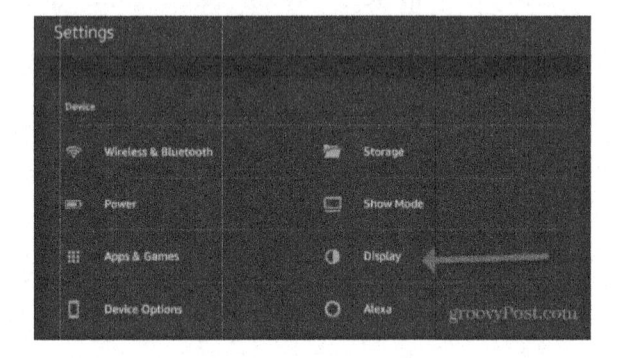

Then click on Display Sleep or Sleep.

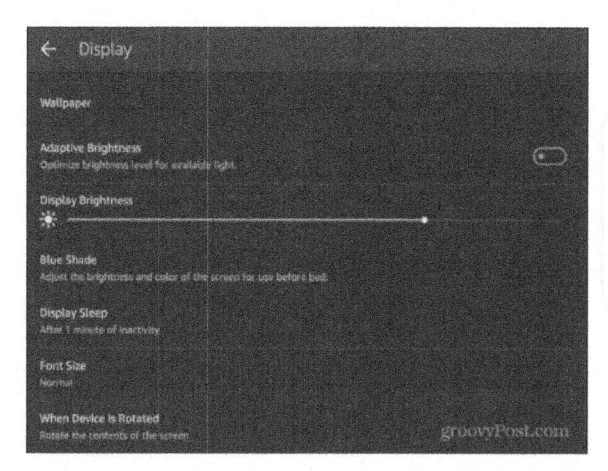

Choose how long, i.e., seconds or minutes, you want your screen to stay on when not using it.

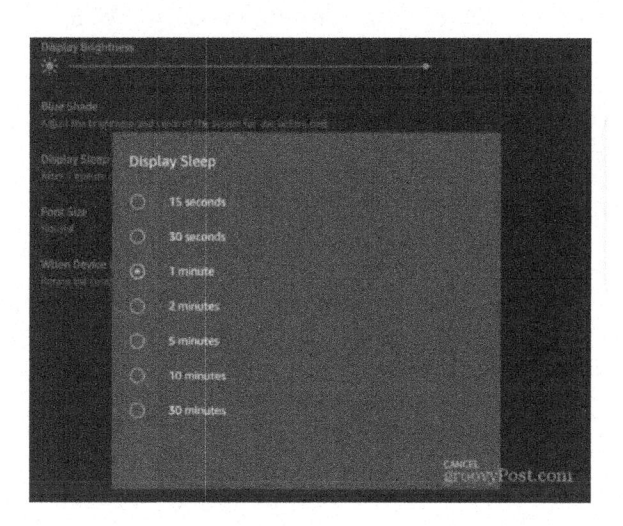

How to Increase And Decrease the Volume?

Unlock the screen and press the volume up or down buttons at the top of the device.

Also, you can go to "Settings"> "Sound & Notification" and set the "Media Volume" or "Sound & Notification Volume" there.

How to Take Screenshots?

To take a screenshot, make sure your Tablet is on the app or webpage you want to take a screenshot.

First, press down the volume down button and quickly tap down the power button, like you are pressing both simultaneously. When the screen flashes and a camera or chime sound is heard, it confirms the Capture.

How to use the Camera?

These steps are helpful if you want to take a photo: Select the Favorites grid and click the Camera app on your home screen.

Click the Camera/Video button.

Hold your Fire tablet and move it around until the image you want to capture is visible.

Click on the Capture button (it is circular and Similar to a camera aperture).

How to Clear Browser History?

1. Scroll down from above the home screen.

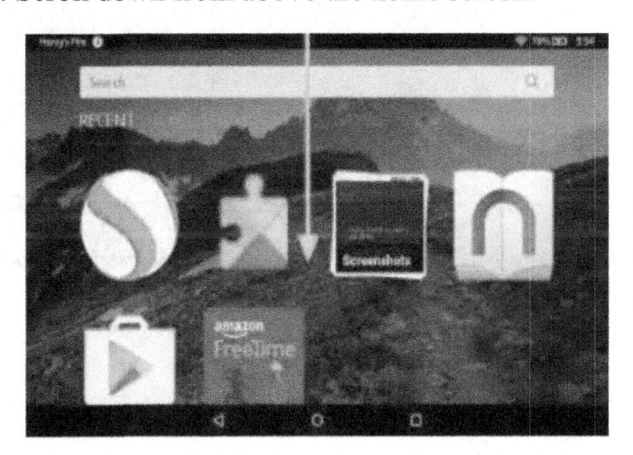

2. Click on Settings.

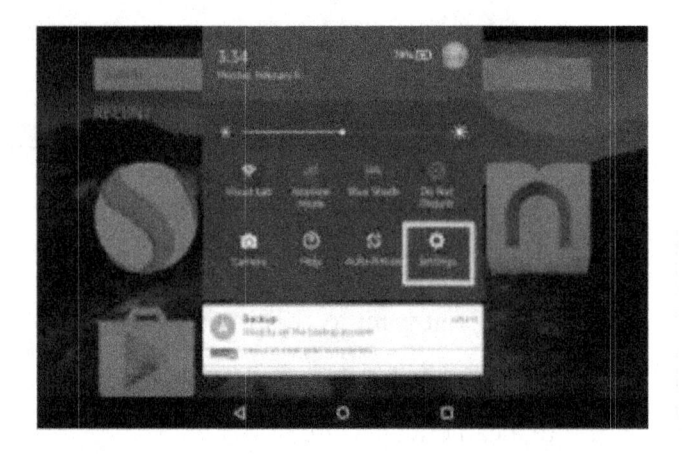

3. Click Apps & Games.

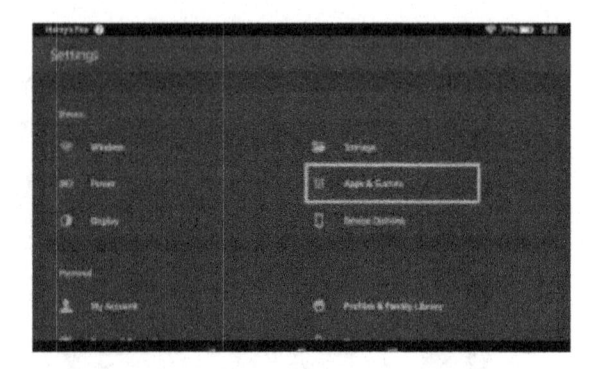

4. Click Amazon Application Settings.

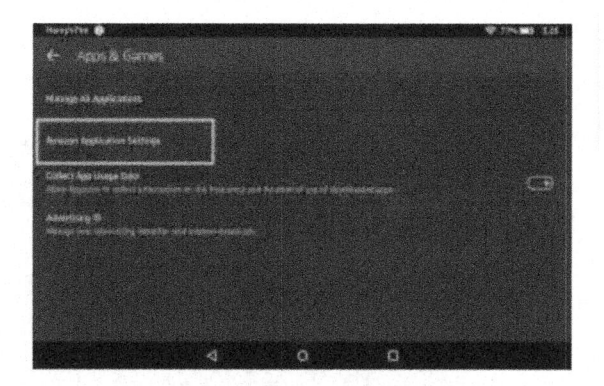

5. Click Silk Browser.

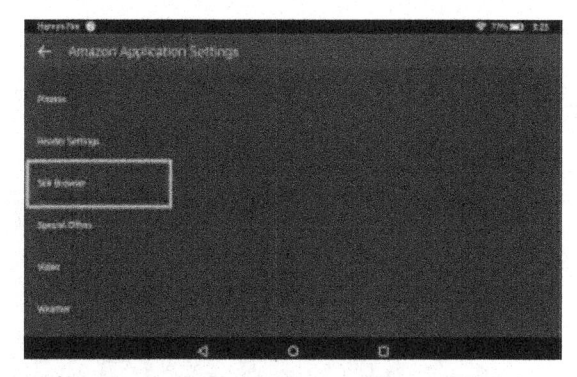

6. Click Privacy.

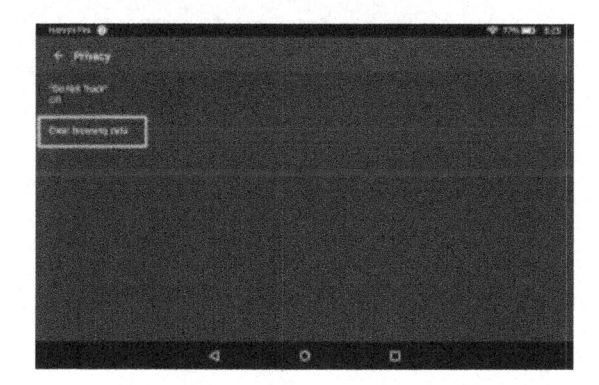

6. Click Clear browsing data.

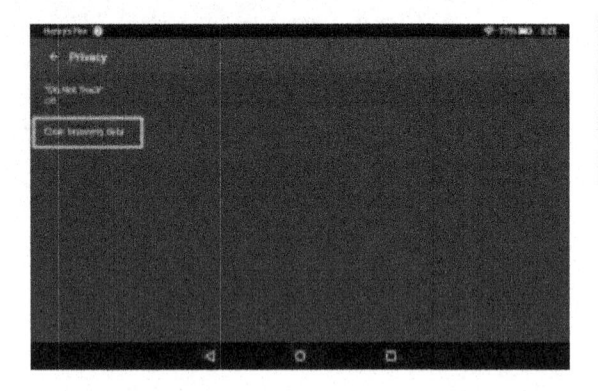

7. Click Clear data. Open the boxes next to Saved Passwords and Autofill form data before you click Clear data to make your tablet cleaner.

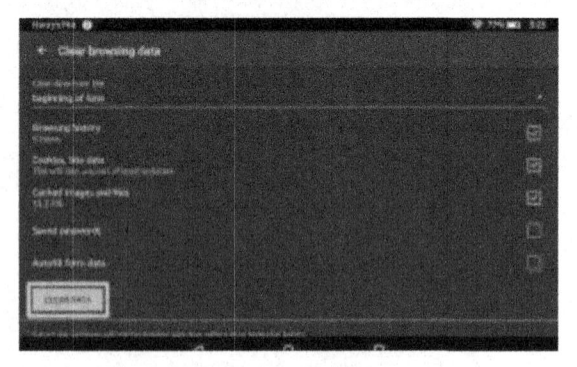

How to Enable Split-Screen?

First of all, open any app and click the 'task switcher, which is the square at the base towards the right of the screen.

Click the app icon at the top, and you will see a slight menu
Tap 'Split Screen.'

The app you were using will be on the left half of the screen. Pick another app that will be on the right half.

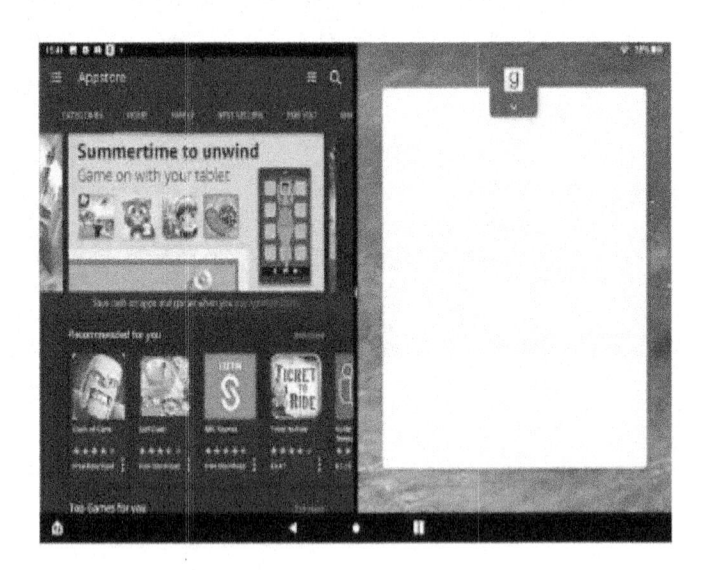

How to Install Software Updates?

Scroll downwards from the top of the screen.

Search for settings in the drop-down menu and click on it.

Select Device Options.

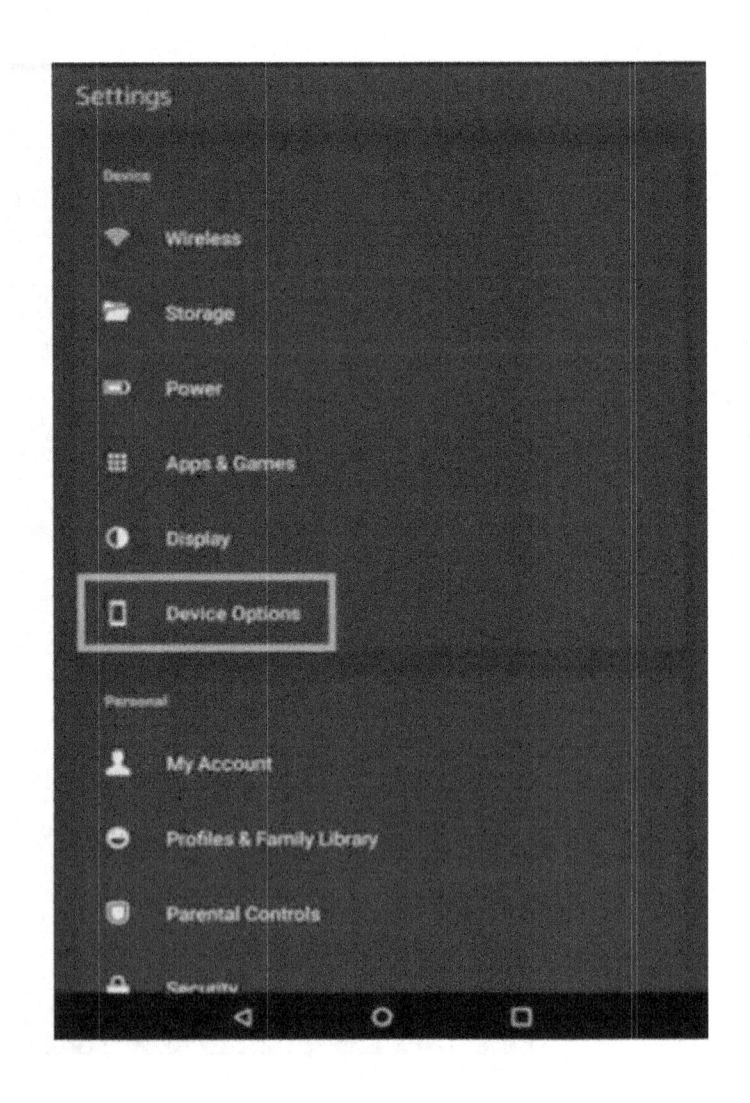

Then click System Updates.

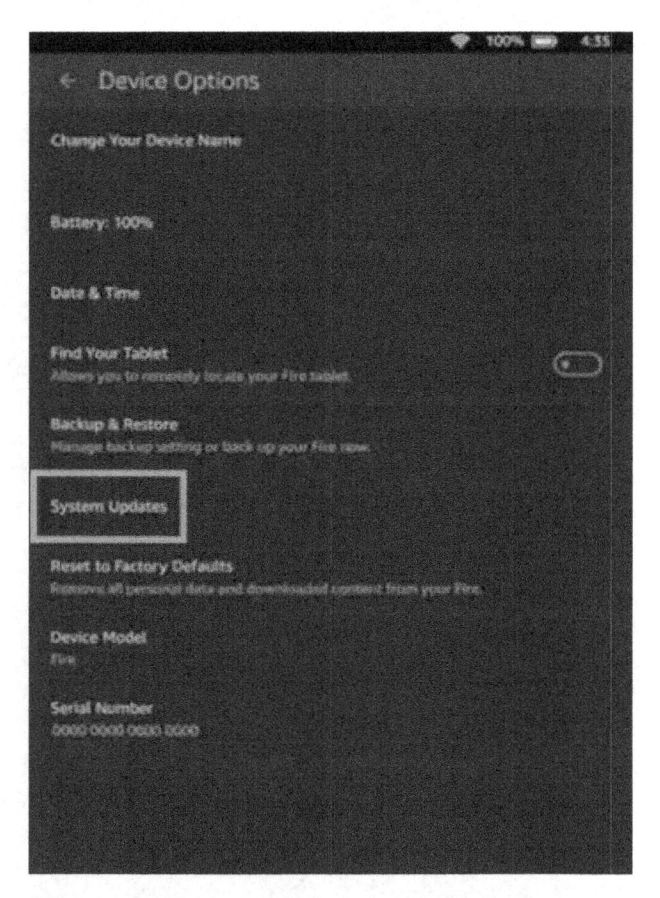

Click check Now.

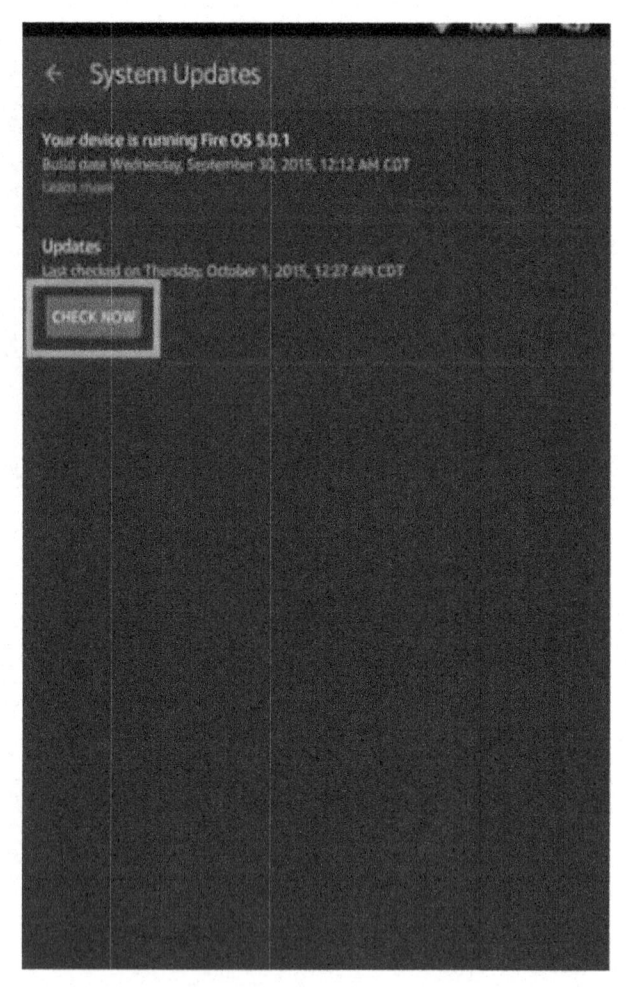

Available updates will be downloaded automatically by the fire tablet.

How to Disable Safe Mode?

Turn the Tablet off. Hold the power button down from the Safe Mode, and tap "Shut Down." wait for the Fire Tablet to switch off completely.

Restart normally. Press and hold the Power button again. When your Fire Tablet restarts, it will be in normal mode.

Chapter 5: HD 10 Tablet Connectivity

How to Connect to The Internet (Wifi On Your Tablet)

If you are connecting a Fire tablet to your wifi network for the first time, do this:

Unlock the Tablet and scroll down on the home screen.

Select wifi and turn it on.

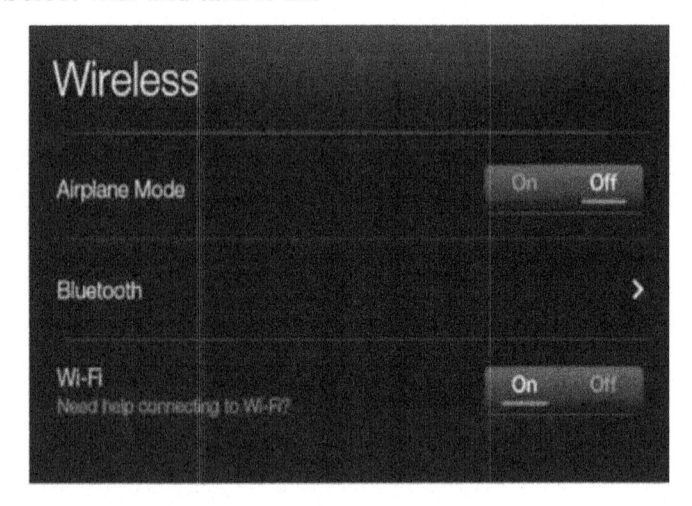

Select your network and select Connect.

Write in the Password to the network.

It may take some time for your Fire to authenticate with your network, and when it is completed, the Fire should connect immediately. It should also recognize the network and automatically log in next time.

Manual Wifi Setup

If your Fire tablet does not automatically connect to your wireless network, you can set it up manually.

Scroll down from the home screen to access Wireless and turn on wifi.

Select Join Other Network.

Type in the name of your network into the Network SSID box.

Click on the right security type from the drop-down menu.

Write the network password and select Save.

If you do not know the network security type, check your router. You will find it on the wireless page. It may be WPA, WPA2-PSK, WPA2-AES, or something similar. Hopefully, it will be WPA2, as when it is WPA, it means your network is insecure.

How to Fix the Authentication Problem?

There are several ways to fix this issue:

Airplane Mode Fix: The Airplane mode provides all device's external (cellular) connections. Activating and then deactivating it may prove to be the quickest fix for the authentication error. It may solve some common issues that might make your device not connect to the wifi. Follow the steps to activate and deactivate this feature.

Select settings and click the "airplane mode" feature. Activate it by tapping on it once.

Then deactivate it by tapping on it again.
Try reconnecting to the wifi

Router: The router may sometimes solve the issue. It just needs to restart to start working again. The following steps help solve this issue.

Unplug your router from the socket for some time and allow it to rest a little.

Plug it back after some time.
Ensure you restart your Tablet by pressing the power button for long.

Now go to the wifi settings.

Click on the network again to re-enter its Password and finish setting up a new connection.

How to Set Time/Date?

Confirm if your device's time/date/Time Zone is correct on your device. This might help solve the problem.

How to Reset the Router?

Resetting the router can also help solve the issue.

Clear the cache

Clearing the device's cache can also help solve the issue.

How to Browse with Your HD 10?

Amazon fire HD 10 comes with Silk, Amazon's web browser, to browse the internet. But Mozilla Firefox is also compatible with Amazon's products, and I can download it.

For a good browsing experience, you will need a solid internet connection and the latest apps on your Tablet.

To use these programs, you only need to open your Tablet, click the icon, and type in your web search.

How to Use the Amazon AppStore?

Scroll to the Home screen and click the "Appstore" icon.

Go through the site and select the app you want, or use the search box at the top of the screen.

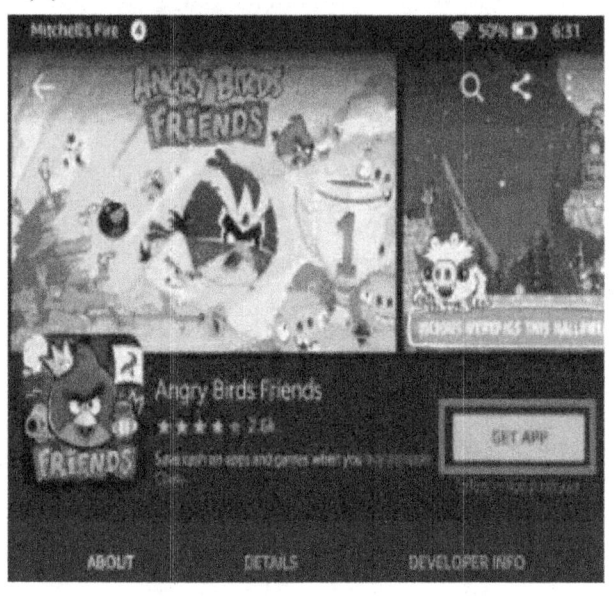

How to Customize Bluetooth Keyboard Shortcuts?

    Click on Settings.

    Click Device options.

    Click on Keyboard & Language.

    Click on Physical Keyboard.

    Click on Email Shortcut Key or Files Shortcut Key, then click any listed app on your device to designate it to the key.

Chapter 6: Registration Of Your New Device

How to Register the Widget on Your Amazon Account?

Register your Tablet in one of these two ways:

Log in with an existing Amazon account – type in your email or mobile number and the Password of your account, then click Continue,

Create a new Amazon account – click Start under the heading "New to Amazon?" and type in the required information, then click Continue.

If you logged in with an account you already have, and you have backed up your data of another Amazon Fire tablet, then you can:

Click Restore to load all your apps and settings from your backup,

Click on Do Not Restore to restart with this Tablet.

How to Pass a Two-step Verification?

Two-Step Verification is a feature that increases the security of your account log-in.

The code and your Password are required for log in/access.

Two-Step Verification sends you a unique security code when you attempt logging in. When you sign up for Two-Step Verification, you can select between receiving the security code by text message or authenticator app.

To enable Two-Step Verification:

In Your Account, click on Login & security.
Click Edit beside Two-Step Verification (2SV) Settings.
Click on Get Started.
Follow the instructions on the screen.

How to Change Your Device Name?

Go to the page to manage Your Content and Devices.

From the Devices tab, click on your device or app.

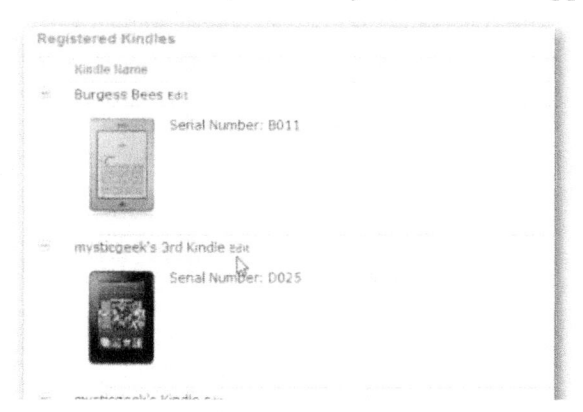

Click on Edit close to the current name.

Write in the name you want and click on Save.

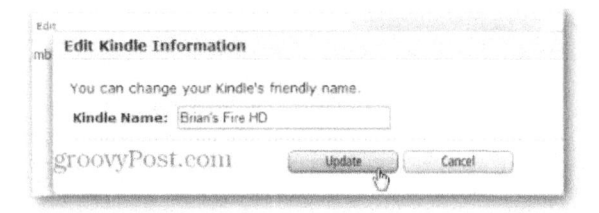

Chapter 7: Charging

How to Wirelessly Charge Your Device?

To charge your Fire HD 10 wirelessly, follow these steps;

Use a Show Dock

Show docks are used to sit your Tablet in the Amazon show mode, but they can also charge your Tablet while doing it.

Try Using a Wireless Qi Receiver

Plug in a Qi receiver into your Tablet's port and place it on a charging pad to wirelessly charge your Tablet.

How to Fix Possible Wireless Charging Issues?

Resetting the Kindle Fire

This can be resolved by rebooting your Fire tablet. Press the "Power" button down for about 20 seconds. Hold down the "Power" button again if the device turns on again. If the Tablet doesn't turn on, plug your charger in and wait for about 15 minutes before turning the power on again.

Checking the Kindle Fire Charger Cable

Check and confirm if the products you are using to charge are guaranteed to be compatible with your Tablet.

Checking the USB Connections

If you are using the correct charging cable to charge your device, check if the USB port has started to come loose, as this can affect the cable's charging ability to transmit power to your device correctly. If the charging port is loose, you will need to get a replacement part.

Making Sure the Power Outlet Works

Ensure that the power outlet you are trying to use is functioning properly.

How to Solve a Liquid Detection Alert?
If a cable is connected to the device and charging, unplug it.

Position the device to face the port side down and shake it gently for at least 5 seconds, or until liquid is not visible in the port.

Place the device on a flat surface for about 48 hours to dry completely.

Chapter 8: Applications

How to Fix Possible App Errors

Reboot your Fire tablet.
Force close the app.
Delete the cache and other data of the app.
Uninstall the app and install it again.
Note: You cannot uninstall apps that are Pre-installed.

How to Force Close An App?

Click on Apps & Games or Apps & Notifications on the Settings menu.
Click on Manage All Applications (if present), then choose the app you want to manage.
Click on Force Stop.

How to Clean An App's Data And Cache

Select the Settings menu.
Click on Apps & Notifications.

Click on Manage All Applications and select the app with issues.

Click on Storage, touch to Clear Data or Clear Storage, then Clear Cache.

How to Move an App On the Screen?

Click and hold the app you want to move for some time.

Drag the app to where you want it to be, or drag it to the top of another app to form a folder

How to Download the Hoopla App?

Select the Play Store and find Hoopla. When you find the app, touch Free. To install the app, Click on Install. When you finish installing, click on the app.

How to Install Tiktok App?

Install the Downloader app, found in the Amazon Appstore for Fire TV devices and the Google Play Store for Android TV devices.

Allow Apps from Unknown Sources. By scrolling to Settings > My Fire TV > Developer Options on Fire TV, you can do this. On Android TV, it's done by scrolling to Settings > Security & Restrictions > Unknown sources.

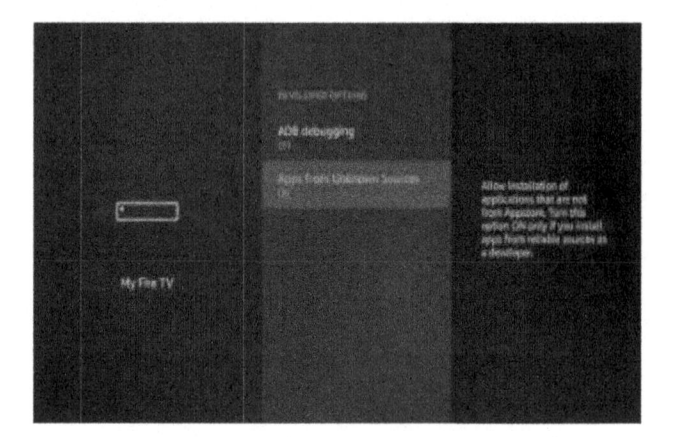

The app will automatically download and remind you to install it. Click on Install, and when you install it, it will appear in your apps list.

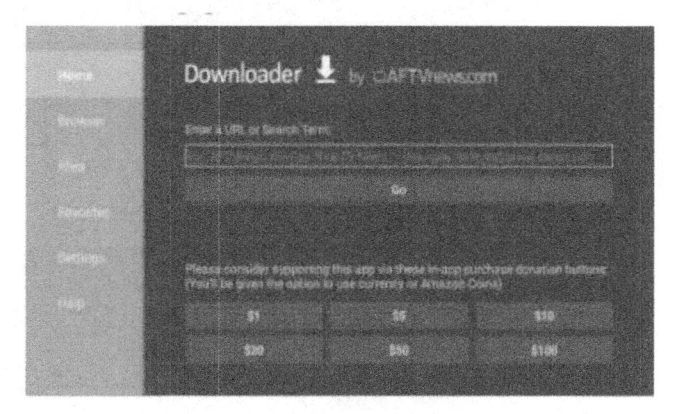

How to install google play store in Amazon Fire HD 10 Tablet

Select the "Settings" app from the "Home" tab on the home screen.

Click on "Settings" on the Home tab.

Navigate to "Security & Privacy."

Click on "Apps From Unknown Sources."

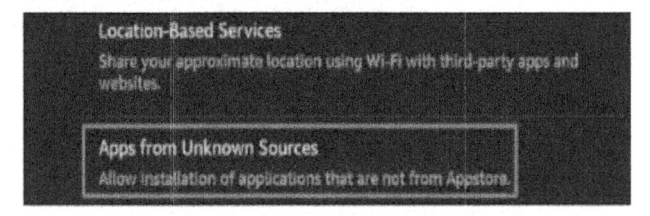

Search for "Silk Browser" and then toggle on "Allow from This Source." This option will help install apps from outside of the Amazon app store.

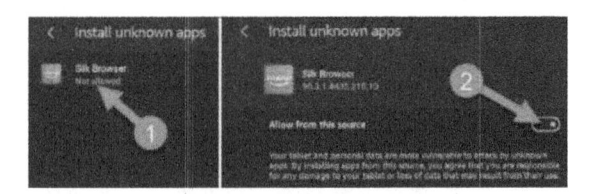

When you finish that, start downloading the Play Store files. There are four APK files specific to your Fire Tablet to help you run your Playstore.

Install the apps in this order; touch the File> click "Continue"> touch the "Install" button. When installed, touch "Done."

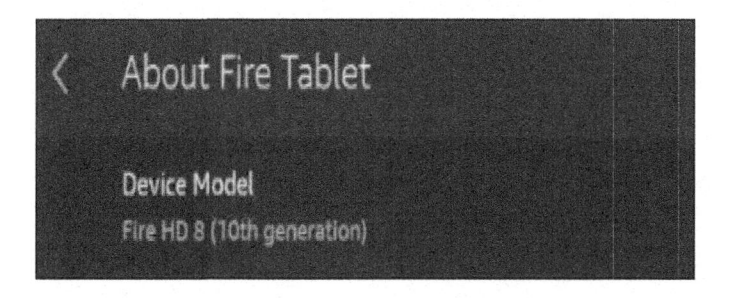

> About Fire Tablet
>
> Device Model
> Fire HD 8 (10th generation)

How to Download an App on Google Playstore?

Select and download apps or digital content.

On your device, select the Google Play Store Google Play or click on the Google Play store on a web browser.

Find or browse for content.

Choose an item.

Click on Install or the price of the item.

Follow the instructions on the screen to finish the transaction and obtain the content.

Chapter 9: Game Mode

How to Enable Game Mode?
Select the Settings menu.

Click on Apps & Games.

Click on Game Mode > On

How to Disable Game Mode ?
Select the Settings menu.

Click on Apps & Games.

Click on Game Mode > Off.

Chapter 10: Print

How to Print From Your Device?

Turn on your printer and connect it to Wi-Fi.

Click on Print from the menu for the item or web page you want to print.

Choose your printer from the list or click on All Printers for close printers.

Choose the number of copies or click on More options to select the size, color, and orientation of paper.
Click on Print.

How to Add a Printer Manually?

Click the menu icon (three vertical dots) or choose the File for the item you want to print, then click on Print.

Click on Save as PDF, then click on All printers

Find the IP address for your printer (check your printer's user guide).

Click on the Add Printer icon (plus sign) to manually add a printer with the printer's IP address.

Chapter 11: Amazon Kindle Guide

How to Download Books from the Amazon Library?

Scroll to the Home page of your Tablet.

Click on Books or open the Kindle app, then click on Library.

To see all the items, you previously purchased, click on all from your Tablet's Library.

Click on the cover of the item you want to retrieve to download it again

Chapter 12: Battery

How Tt Conserve Battery Power?
- Force close background.
- Dim your screen.
- Reduce the timeout of your device.
- Check if your device is working on the latest software version.
- With Smart Suspend, disconnect from your network when not using it.
- Reduce the volume or use headphones.
- Activate Battery Saver or Low Power Mode.

What is Smart Suspend?

This feature helps manage the power consumption on your Fire tablet. The Smart Suspend feature is informed of when you use your device and automatically turns on and off your Internet connection depending on the expected usage. Automatic Smart Suspend is turned on by default and is managed from the settings.

How to Turn on Battery Saver?

- Click on Battery in Settings.
- Click on Low Power Mode to manually turn on the battery saver and increase your Tablet's battery life.

Chapter 13: Household Profiles

How to Create a Child Profile?

Click on settings

Navigate to the "Personal" section and click Profiles & Family Library.

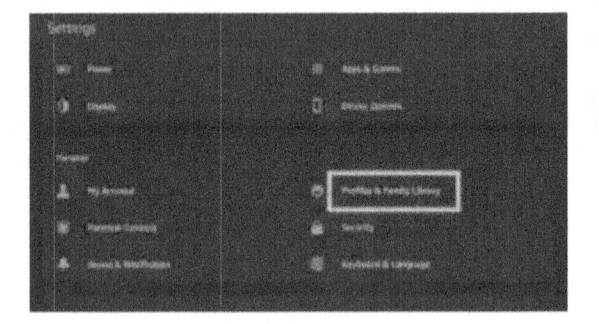

Click on Add a child profile.

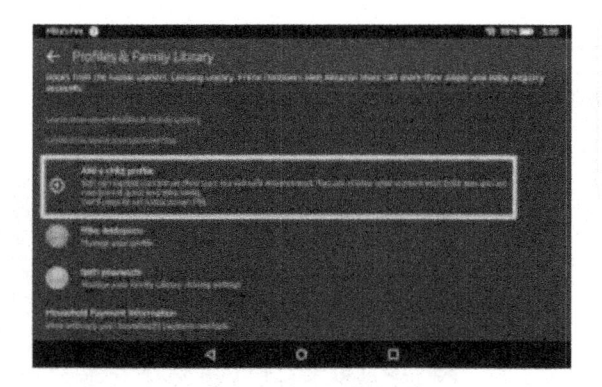

Click on PIN or Password,

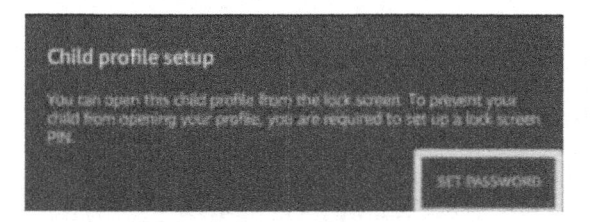

Type in the PIN or Password again and click on Finish.

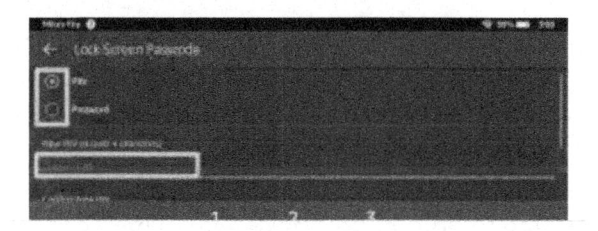

Write the child's first name where prompted. Click on select a profile picture if you want to do that.

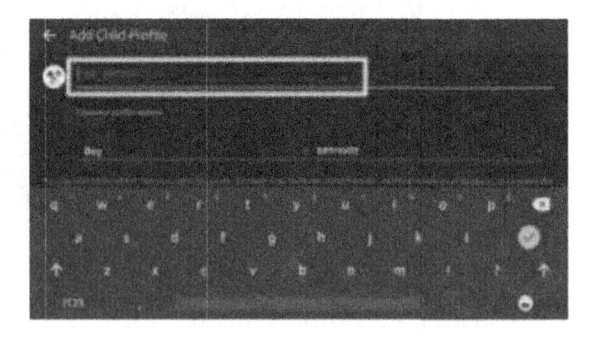

Touch Boy to choose a gender and click on Birthdate to type in their date of birth.

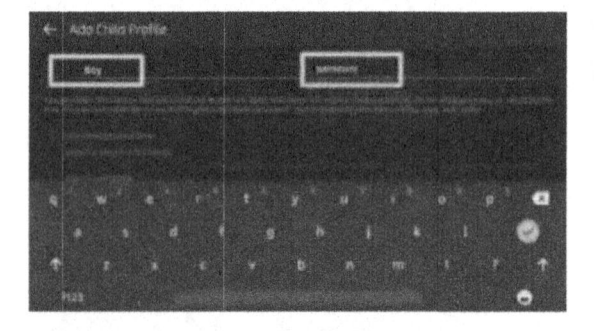

Select either Use Amazon FreeTime or Use Teen Profiles and click on Add Profile. The Fire will select one for you according to your child's birth date, which can be changed.

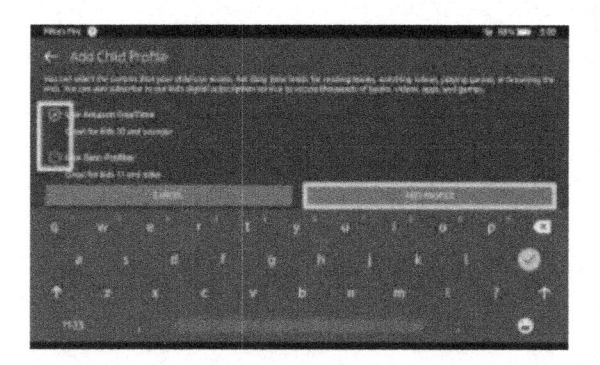

After this, you will see a screen that allows you to add content from your collection to that profile. Click on Done when you finish. The first tab is the amazon content suitable for children, labeled Kid Friendly.

If you have not signed in before, you will be prompted to sign up for FreeTime Unlimited.

Click on Enable Browser to get the FreeTime Web Browser, which only allows kids to access content that Amazon believes to be age-appropriate.

View the boxes close to child profiles to grant browser access rights, and click on Done.

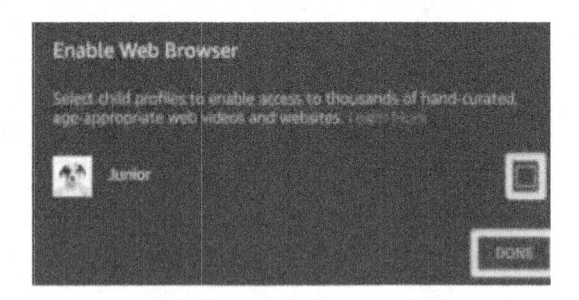

Click on OK to accept that the Fire tablet uses filters to know which web pages and FreeTime Unlimited content are right.

You have completed your child's profile. Please turn off the Enable Web Browser switch so your child from re access it.

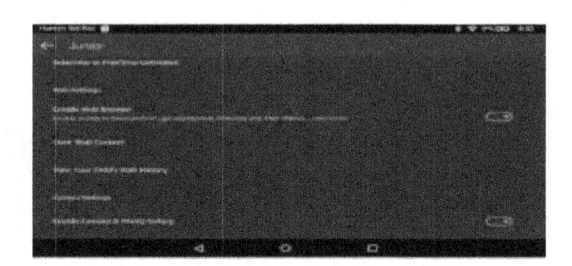

Chapter 14: Parental Control

What is a Parental Control?

Parental control is a feature that allows you to reduce access to Web browsing: email, Contacts, and Calendar apps. You are buying from the Amazon Store.

How to Enable Parental Control?
- Scroll down from above the screen and click Settings.
- Touch Parental Controls.
- Touch the switch close to Parental Controls.
- Write a password and confirm it.
- Click Finish.
- When the parental controls are on, you will see a lock icon at the top of the screen.

How to Adjust Communication Features?
- Navigate to the Parent Dashboard.
- Click on the Settings icon close to the child's name.
- Below the Fire Tablet Settings, click on Manage Communications.
- To grant your child access to communication features, select Grant parental consent and follow the instructions on the screen. Or, if you want the features to be hidden from your, select Hide these features on Fire tablet.
- After you grant access, find the available features you want to activate for your child.

How to Approve Contact for Your Child?

- Click on the Alexa app.
- Click on Communicate.
- Click on the contacts icon.
- Click on your name.
- Click on your child's name.
- Click on Add New Contact.

Chapter 15: Data Storage

How to run microSD on your Tablet?

Fix your MicroSD card in the slot,

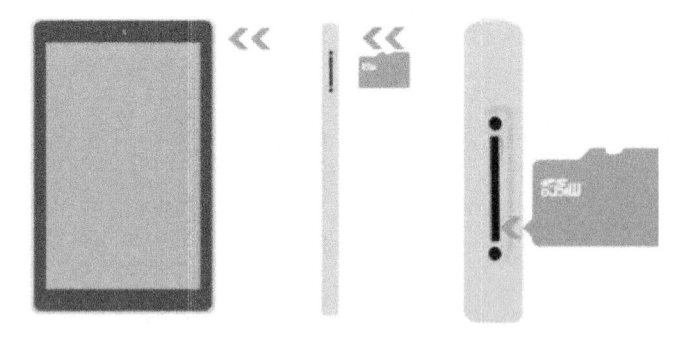

You will be prompted that whatever you download from now onwards will be saved to the card.

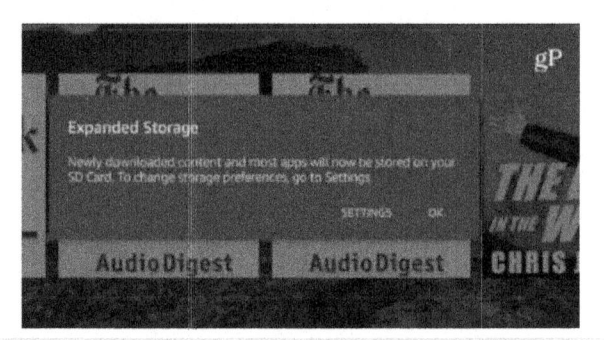

How to Delete all Data from Your SD Card?

Click on Storage from the Settings menu.

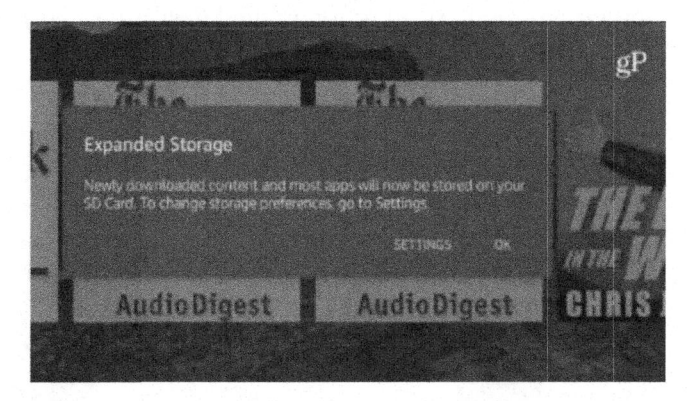

Click on Erase SD Card to clear all data on your microSD card.

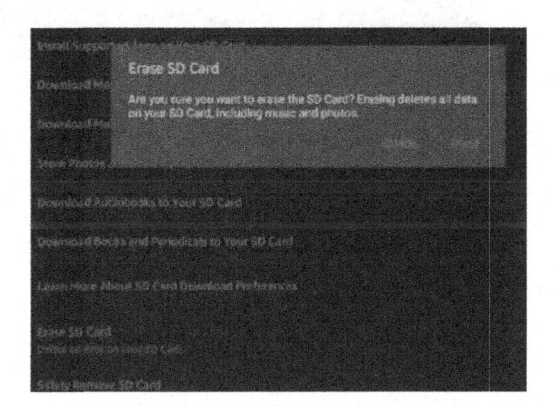

Chapter 16: Alexa

How to use Device Dashboard?

To access the new Device Dashboard from your Fire tablet screen, you only need to touch the latest Smart Home button on the left side of the navigation bar.

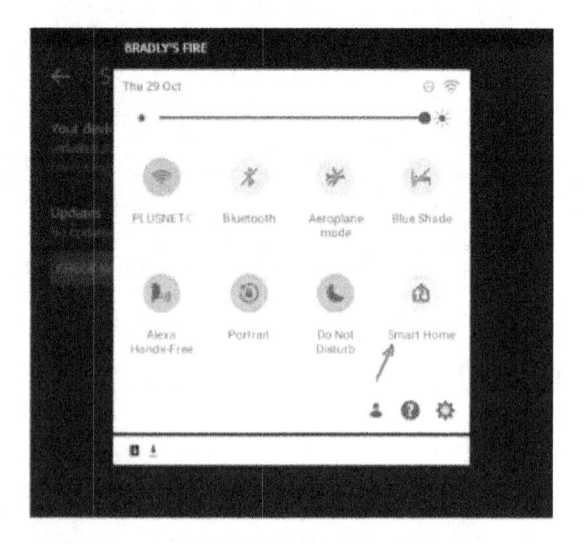

How to Connect Smart Home Devices to Alexa?
- Select the Alexa app on your Tablet.
- Click on Smart Home Devices.
- Click on Add.
- Click on Add Device.
- Select your device category.

- Click on your device brand.
- Follow the on-screen instructions to link your smart home device to Alexa.

How to use Alexa on Your Tablet?

- From your Home screen, navigate to the right until the Apps page is visible and then find "Alexa."
- Download the Amazon Alexa app.
- When it installs automatically, touch Amazon Alexa on your Home screen to launch it.
- Write your name and click on Continue.

How to Enable Alexa Hands-free?

To activate or deactivate Alexa hands-free, scroll down from the top of the home screen and click on the Alexa Hands-Free icon. If there is a PIN or Password set on your device, certain features of Alexa require that you type in the Password or PIN.

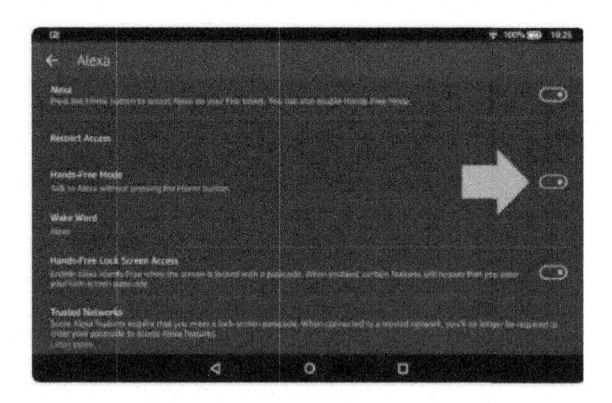

How to Permanently Disable Alexa?

Alexa cannot be uninstalled, but you can turn it off. When the home is held, you can stop Alexa from coming up by going to Settings>Device Options and searching for the Alexa title, then touch the slider to make it so that Alexa would not come up when the home is held.

How to Switch to Show Mode?

Scroll down from your Tablet's home screen above and touch the Show Mode toggle to activate Show Mode. Or you can say, "Alexa, switch to Show Mode."

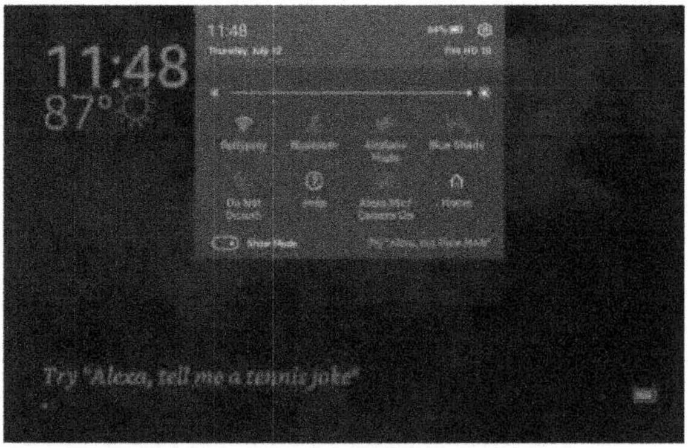
11:48
87°
11:48
Try "Alexa, tell me a tennis joke"

Chapter 17: Data Reset

How to Reset Your Tablet to Factory Setting?
Scroll down twice from above the screen to make Quick Settings visible.

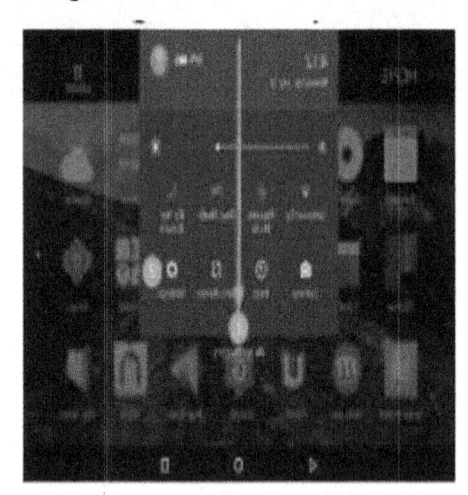

Touch the Settings icon. Click on Device Options,

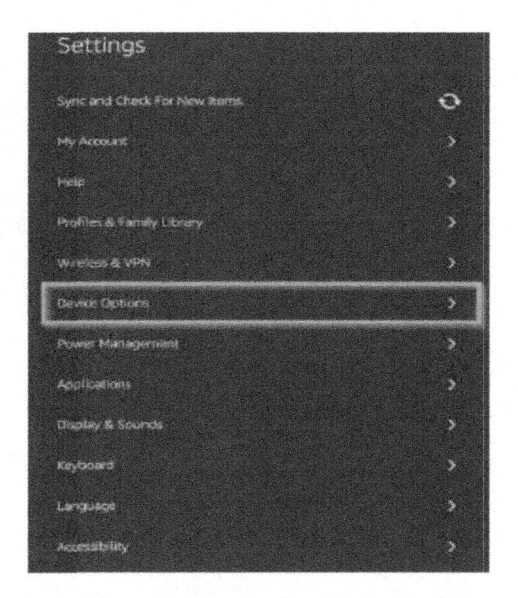

And then click on Reset to Factory Defaults.

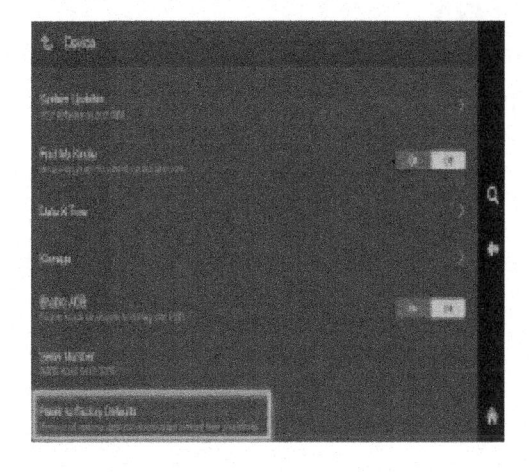

And click on reset to confirm

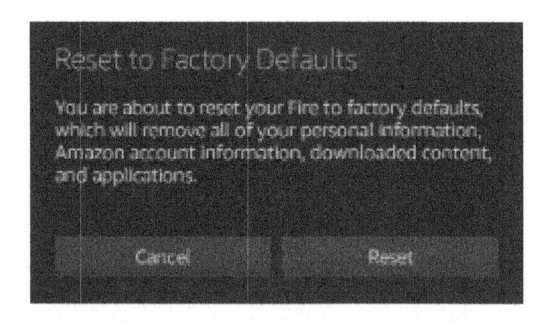

How to Soft Reset Your Tablet?
Touch and hold the "Volume Down" and "Power" buttons together for 10 seconds till the device shuts down.

How to Reset Lock Screen Password or Parental Controls PIN?
If you forgot your parental controls password, you can reset it easily from the home screen.

To Reset Your Parental Controls Password:

Scroll down from above your screen, and click on the Parental Controls notification.

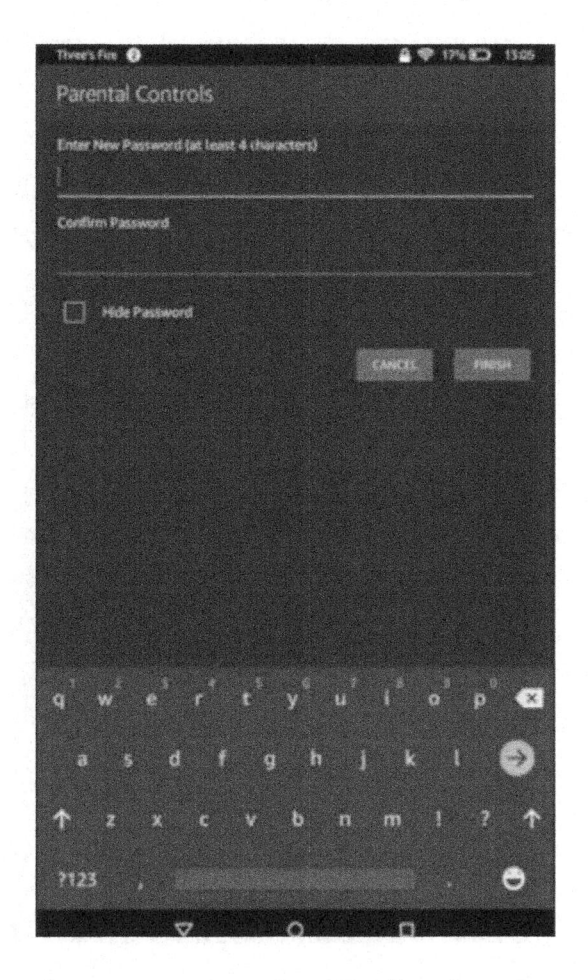

Type in an incorrect password or PIN five times in a row to see the popup, and click on the Reset your Parental Controls Password message.

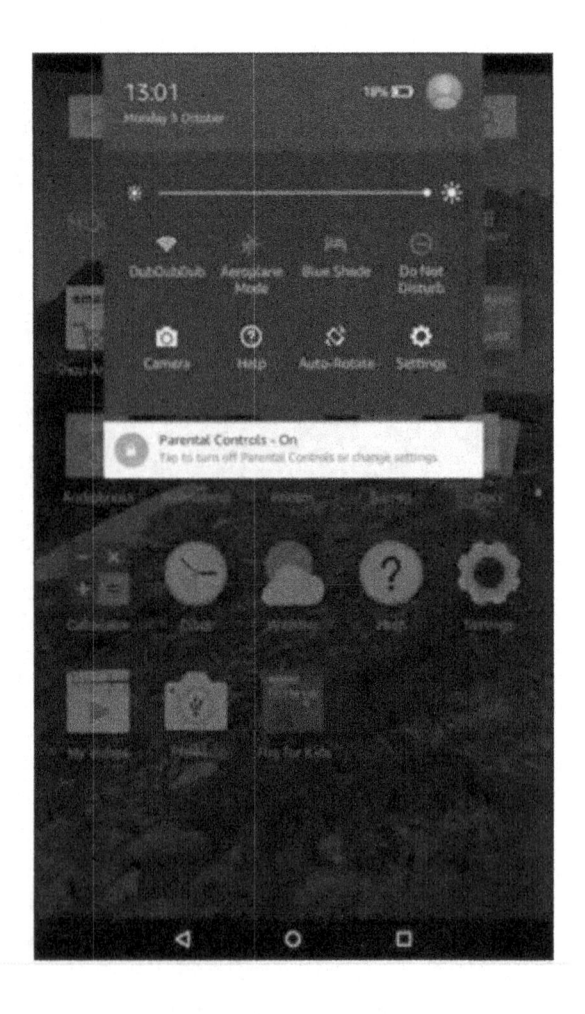

Now, you need to sign in to your Amazon account. Type in your account password and click Continue.

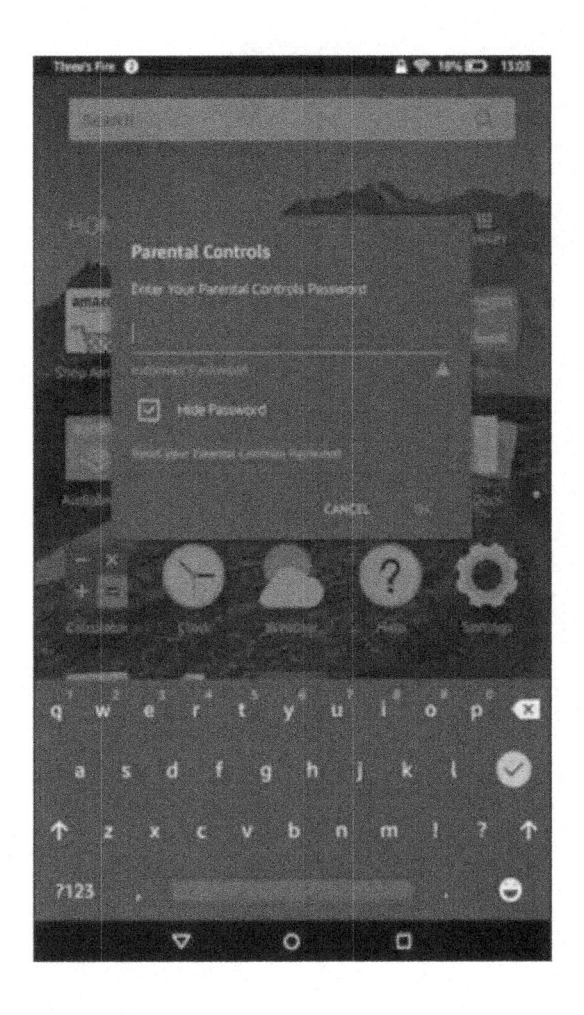

Type in a parental controls password that is different from the old one, and touch Finish.

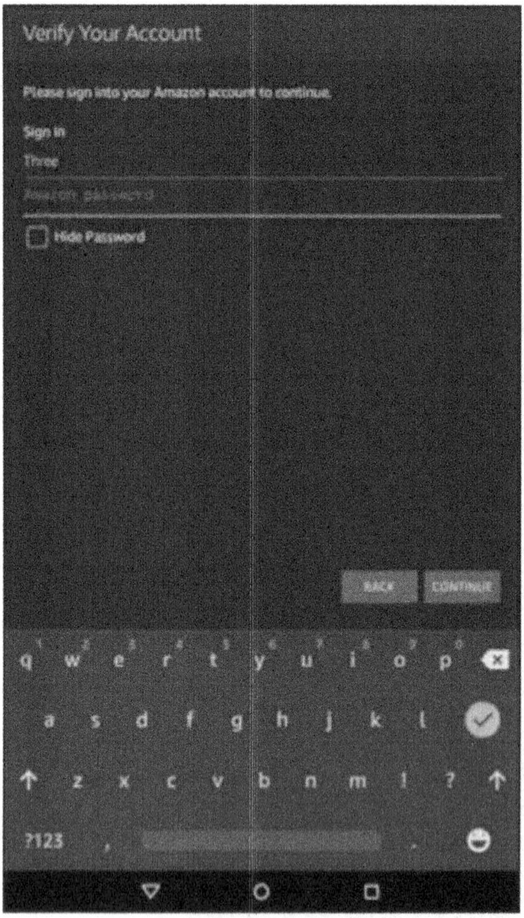
Verify Your Account
Please sign into your Amazon account to continue.
Sign in
Hide Password

Chapter 18: ADS

Where is Ads Usually Shown?

>Ads are shown as screensavers when your device is in sleep mode and below your device's home screen. On Fire tablets, you will see them on the lock screen.

How to Remove Ads from Your Tablet?
Log in to your Amazon account.

Go through Accounts and Lists and tap Account.

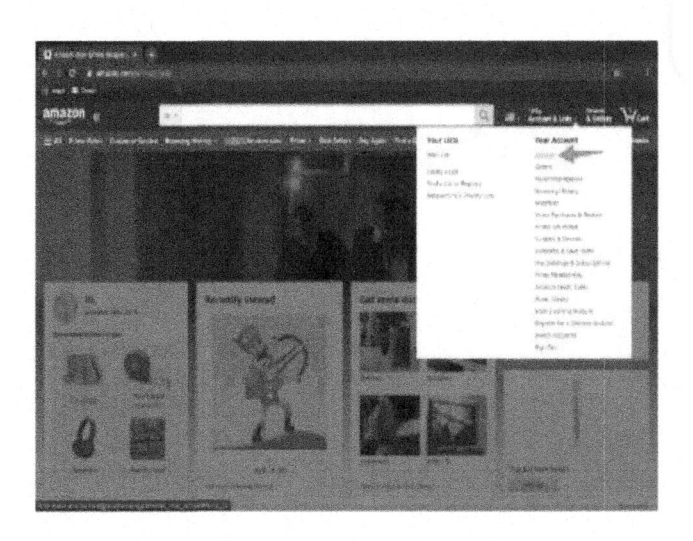

Select Your devices and content.

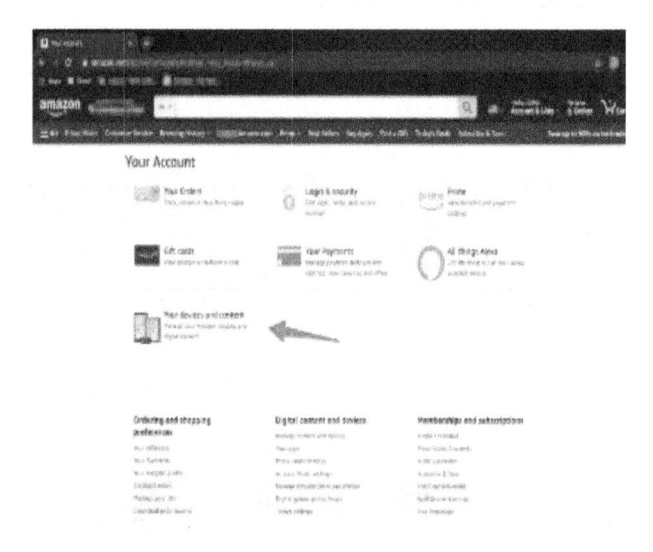

Select Manage Devices.

114 | Page

Select and then tap registered Fire Tablet.

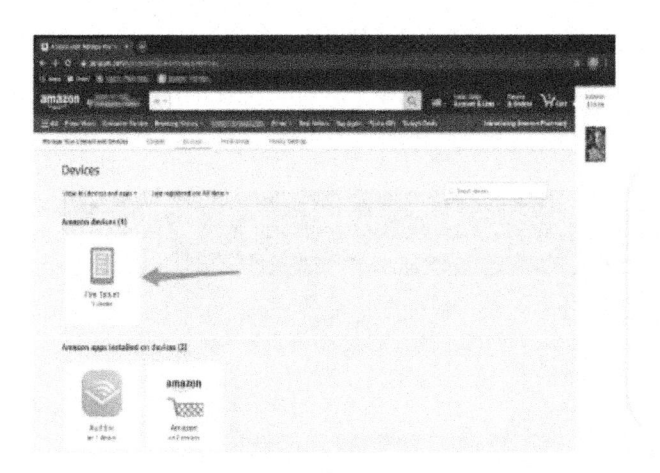

On the Special Offers section, click on Remove offers.

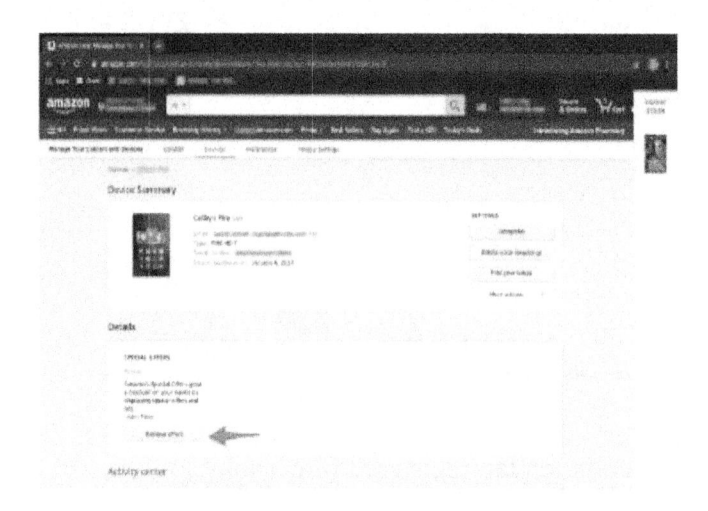

Tap End offers and Pay the Fee.

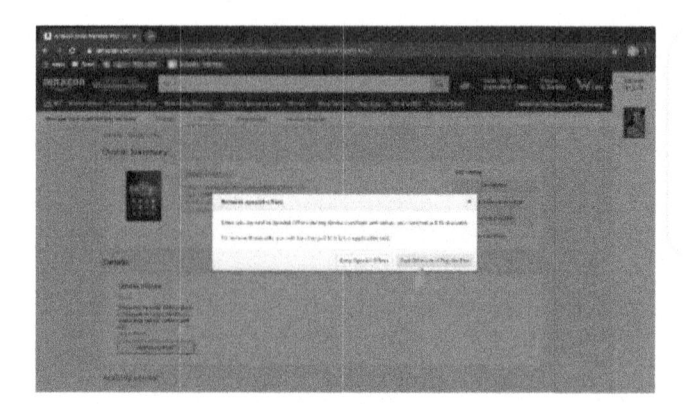

Chapter 19: Troubleshooting Tips & Tips

How to Fix a Massive Battery Drain Issue

- Soft reset.
- Uninstall unknown apps.
- Factory reset your Fire Tablet.
- Turn your fire tablet when you are not using it.
- Use automatic smart suspend.
- Turn the battery saver feature on.
- Use Airplane mode.

How to fix the stuck kindle Logo?

- Tap and hold the Power button for 40 seconds.
- If the device restarts in less than 40 seconds, release the Power button.

How to fix Constant Shutting Down Issue?

A low battery can sometimes make your Tablet randomly go off. Plug your device in and leave it to charge for about 50%. When it charges above this point, reboot the Tablet to solve the issue. Tap and hold your Fire HD 10's power button to power the device off.

How to fix the "An Internal Error Occurred" issue?

"An internal Error Occurred" issue can result from a lack of network connectivity, so ensure the network connection is good. Another solution is to deregister your Tablet by swiping from the top of the screen to the bottom.

How to fix Overheating Issue?

Too busy CPU: close the open applications on the Amazon Fire HD one after the other and observe if the Tablet cools down.

Suppose the Amazon Fire HD overheats while charging: use the original charging cable if you still have it. If not, use another cable.

When the Battery overheats: install a temperature control app that can regulate the Amazon Fire HD battery. If it persists, replace the Battery so it doesn't explode.

If the ambient temperature is way too high, close the applications and take your Amazon Fire HD far from the sun when it is cooled.

If you request too much power: Take video games or activities break.

How to Fix the Battery Charging Issue?

- Testing The Charging Adapter, Cable & Port.
- Ensure that the outlet your charger is plugged in has an active charge.
- To confirm if the charger has a fault, attach the USB cable to a computer or other power source to try charging it. If it sets, then the charger has a fault.
- Make sure the cable is seated securely When connecting it. Try moving it around gently to check for signs of a loose connector. Try laying your Fire on a flat surface while charging it if this is the case. If your tablet charges after this, the issue is with the port leading to your Amazon Fire tablet.

Try Resetting your Tablet

Only do this if other methods fail to produce positive results. This wipes out everything you pre-loaded to your Tablet and returns it to its default configuration. But we are not sure if it will solve the issue.

If all the above methods do not work, try replacing the Battery.

How to Fix the Issue with Sound Not Coming Through Speakers/Headphones?

- Check the Volume Level on Your Fire.
- Try using Headphones and the Built-in Speaker.
- Check the headphones. Seating.
- Try using a Different Pair of Headphones.
- Try cleaning the Headphones, Jack.
- Test Different Media.
- Restart your Tablet

Conclusion

The Amazon Fire HD 10 is a particular device and a piece of hardware. It has a low-quality display quality when compared to other devices. But it is a compelling product for the correct type of user.

Amazon Fire HD 10 is budget-friendly. It has high quality and better warranties than its competitors. It also has a more powerful processor, higher RAM, and Fire OS 7 for better performance than older Fire models.

The Fire HD 10 has dual speakers with Dolby Atmos branding. The audio quality is not too high, tinny, and hollow but loud enough to fill a room. Bluetooth 4.2 and a headphone jack are present for alternate listening options.

Amazon Fire HD 10 is not as fast as the Apple iPad but is relatively quick compared to other fire tablets.

2MP cameras are present at the front and back of the Tablet, but they are somehow blurry and noisy.

Generally speaking, Amazon Fire HD 10 is the best 10-inch Tablet available for $150. It functions faster, has a higher-resolution display, and has a much higher battery life than the HD 8. Presently, there aren't any Android tablets suitable for the size and price of Amazon hd10. If you are going for a different tablet that is better than this, it will cost more than twice two. So if you want a simple, media-focused, and affordable tablet, the Fire HD 10 is the best choice.